By Edmond Cahn

*The Moral Decision*
*The Sense of Injustice*
*The Predicament of Democratic Man*

# *The Predicament of Democratic Man*

*Edmond Cahn*

A DELTA BOOK • 1962

*To My Beloved Wife*

*"Many women have done valiantly,
But thou excellest them all."*

*A Delta Book*
PUBLISHED BY
DELL PUBLISHING CO., INC.
750 THIRD AVENUE
NEW YORK 17, NEW YORK

BY ARRANGEMENT WITH THE MACMILLAN COMPANY
LIBRARY OF CONGRESS CATALOG CARD NUMBER: 61–10343
MANUFACTURED IN THE UNITED STATES OF AMERICA
COVER ILLUSTRATION BY PETER MAX
THIRD PRINTING

# *Contents*

# I

# *The Predicament and Its Background*

# I

# *The Purpose of This Book*

In this present era that tests all systems and challenges all assumptions, it is time to recognize the truth about our new moral condition. We are the citizens and voters of the free nations. For two centuries or more, we have been proclaiming that the people are the exclusive source of political authority and that their consent is the foundation of the powers of government. In order to define the people's consent and raise it to the level of an active mandate, we have been steadily extending and expanding the right of franchise. Solemnly we insist that citizens are the ultimate sovereigns in whose name and by whose authority every official act is performed. The legislators, executives, and administrators whom we select and guide by our votes are assumed to represent no one but us; they speak in our stead and act for our account. In this condition, if an official act should happen to be brutally unjust, who might be considered responsible for it?

Let me put a concrete instance. Not long ago a couple of masked bandits entered a store in a large American city, pointed their guns at the woman who owned the store, and demanded the contents of the cash register. It happened that a policeman was visiting her at the time. When the bandits saw the policeman, they shot and killed him, took the money, and disappeared. Incensed by the murder of one of their comrades, the police rounded up a number of unemployed young men of the neighborhood. The woman identified two of them as the burglars. Although they protested their innocence and offered credible evidence that they were elsewhere at the time of the crime, the district attorney prosecuted them zealously, the jury believed the woman's testimony, and on their being convicted for the robbery and killing, the judge sentenced them to ninety-nine years in the penitentiary.

One of the young men, whom I shall call only by his first name, Joe, had come from Poland to America as a baby in the arms of his mother, Tillie. After Joe's conviction had been affirmed on appeal and all hope of legal redress had been abandoned, it was Tillie, a simple scrubwoman, who caused the truth to come to light. She posted a newspaper advertisement offering a reward of $5,000, which represented eleven years of savings from scrubbing floors. The advertisement intrigued newspaper reporters, who began investigating and soon discovered that the entire prosecution had been baseless.

The prosecution's key witness, the woman who owned the store, had originally refused to identify the two defendants. She had changed her testimony and identified them only because the police, knowing that she had been selling liquor illegally, had threatened to send her to jail if she did not lie as they demanded. But the conspiracy was not confined to the police; at its apex stood the district attorney. Why had he been so eager for a conviction and so ruthless in securing one? Because, at the time of the crime, a great international exposition was about to open in the city, and visitors and customers must be reassured that the prosecutor and police were efficient and the streets of the city entirely safe.

After these facts were exposed in the newspaper, public clamor brought it about that the two young men were pardoned and released. By then, of course, the exposition was long since over, and the district attorney had been honored at many community meetings and lawyers' banquets, had received the usual certificates, tributes, resolutions, and diplomas, had eaten and digested his meals, smoked and enjoyed his cigars, and delivered solemn speeches at his church.

What shall we say is new about this case in terms of our own moral condition? Surely men have been imprisoned, tortured, and executed for crimes they did not commit as far back as we can trace the history of law to the very dawn of politically organized society. In innumerable instances where a crime was actually committed, the wrong person has been punished; in innumerable other instances, a person has been punished though no crime at all was committed and the judicial authorities were either deceived or chose to be deceived in upholding a baseless accusation. The disaster befell Joe and his mother Tillie because it was convenient for the city and its merchants that someone, almost anyone, be found, identified, and convicted. We must concede that most of the pattern is very old, older than the Bible. It is older than the death that came to Uriah the Hittite because a king desired to possess Uriah's wife, or the death that came to Naboth because another king desired to possess Naboth's vineyard, and there is no comforting reason to believe that any city or state is today immune from incidents of the kind.

Certainly, there was little novelty in Joe's position. In all probability, no one—not even the district attorney—hated Joe personally, at least at the start. True, Joe's catastrophe did have some special aspects, which he may have considered rather important. It happened that at the time when Joe was accused of the crime, his wife was expecting a child, which was born during the course of the prosecution. After Joe had been convicted and the conviction affirmed by the highest court, and after a long time had passed during which he remained in the penitentiary, he and his wife agreed that she should divorce him and marry a friend of theirs so that the child might have a normal home and family. All this was carried out before Tillie had saved enough money to offer a reward. Though Joe may have attached special importance to the circumstances, it is improbable that they were in any sense unusual in the annals of legal systems.

Who will contend that there was anything novel about Tillie's behavior? Mothers have always defended their sons on every continent and in every age, and if the case is exceptional at all, it must be because Joe happened to be as innocent as Tillie believed him. In all probability, all she needed was his unsupported assertion that he was innocent. She could not have been influenced by mountains of evidence to the contrary. Moreover, being completely unacquainted with the shibboleths and slogans of popular psychology, she did not even have to fear that she was yielding to an Oedipus complex.

As all of the factors in Joe's and Tillie's condition were old and familiar, so are most of the factors in our own. It has always been possible for the members of a society to project themselves imaginatively—as we do now—into the place of a victim of legal oppression and share the impact of his experience. This capacity to identify ourselves with him has great survival value for us as well as for him. Our personal impulse for safety and self-preservation becomes active the moment we realize that what has happened to him may in turn happen to us if we should be caught in the toils of a similar mischance.

In some instances, there is also a higher, more unselfish level which our identification may reach. On this level, we become eager to save Joe, not because of any collateral or contingent threat to our own safety but because any harm to Joe as a specimen of the genus homo inflicts immediate harm on all mankind, and as our larger self encompasses Joe, his injury automatically becomes ours. On this level, we are not so much preoccupied with the possibility that we may some day stand in the prisoner's dock. We are more preoccupied with the fact that we already stand there—in Joe's person.

Yet, all these things were true long before the rise of modern representative democracy, and were known to the wise men of ancient times. The new factor is quite different. It is not that we find ourselves identified with either Joe or Tillie. It is that, increasingly since the beginning of the modern period, we citizens find ourselves identified with the oppressive district attorney. Representative government has implicated us. It has made us participants—accomplices, if you will—in the deeds that are done in our name and by our authority. Since we are the principals whom the district attorney represents as agent, we feel somehow and to some degree linked and tied to the consequences of his behavior. Without intending anything of the sort, we have wandered into the circle of responsibility. As human beings, it has always been possible to connect ourselves with the victim of wrong; as citizens, our growing dilemma is that we find ourselves unexpectedly connected with the inflicter of wrong. *The new predicament of democratic man is his moral involvement in the misdeeds of government.*

This vicarious involvement of ours is almost sure to feel disconcerting and unwelcome when we confront it squarely for the first time. It can seem all the more disturbing when officers of government perpetrate an act of wrong within our own boundaries, in the course of our own public affairs, within the walls, as it were, of our national house. The things our representatives do in foreign lands are easier for conscience to shrug off; if a wrong is committed abroad, we can usually find some specious way to blame the perverse foreign populace or their wicked rulers or the regrettable lack of an international moral order or perhaps the dire necessities of modern warfare. But all such excuses fail completely whenever officials commit an injustice on our community threshold and implicate us in a strictly domestic operation. At home the legal system, the social influences, and the moral order are no one else's but ours. That is why the true shape of the democratic predicament is not to be found there, overseas, but here, on our doorstep, in cases as simple and stark as Tillie's and Joe's.

The purpose of this book is threefold:

Part One. To explain the nature and background of our moral involvement in the wrongs of government;

Part Two. To demonstrate by rational analysis that the vicarious guilts and responsibilities, which we are accustomed to dread because they loom so large in their present vagueness, are not in fact too burdensome for us but, on the contrary, are quite definable and tolerable; and further

Part Three. To show the dynamic incentives of democratic existence which reduce the weight of our responsibilities, augment our moral power to bear them, and make our total condition not merely tolerable but uniquely desirable.

It is a necessary enterprise we embark on. If despite our best efforts we do not succeed in one respect or another, we shall at least have posed some of the elemental questions of the age. Our undertaking belongs to all citizens of the free world, and few will wish to stand aloof.

# II

# *The Background in Democratic Thinking*

## *Outgrown Allegories of the State*

For generations we of the world's free nations have been moving into a new realm of being as we instituted representative forms of government and proceeded to extend and universalize the right of suffrage. It is unimportant to say just when the process began; scholars may contend as they please for the date of some event in English or American or perhaps Swiss political history. What really matters is that we have been testing a variety of new powers, and find them to be strangely limited. What matters even more is that we have sensed the burden of new moral involvements and know virtually nothing about their limits.

In his late years, Thomas Jefferson, recognizing that representative government had begun something intrinsically novel in human experience, went so far as to recommend our dismissing Aristotle as a preceptor of democratic societies, because like other classical philosophers he had dealt with democracy mainly in the "pure" or direct form which was impracticable beyond the limits of a town. Though the ancients may have had sound ideas on the value of personal liberty, Jefferson thought they could not guide men concerning the structure of a free *representative* government.

He concluded, "The full experiment of a government democratical but representative was and is still reserved for us."

As democratic experiments still continue a century and a half after Jefferson, and their moral implications continue to emerge, we cannot escape wondering where they are taking us. We cannot escape asking: When and how far does representative government involve or implicate us in its injuries and wrongs? The question will not brook evasion. There may have been reason for Aristotle and Jefferson to remain silent on the subject, for one of them did not know the modern system of representation and the other saw only its uncertain beginnings. Our situation is quite different; the question of responsibility confronts us in all its ominous vagueness. Again and again during the past century, we have seen some despot or other ruthlessly exploiting this selfsame vagueness to implicate an entire nation in his political crimes—by holding a rigged popular election, a theatrically fraudulent trial, or a plebiscite of pretended ratification. It is the demagogues, above all, who have understood precisely how civic anxiety arises and how it may be manipulated to destroy civil freedoms.

Why the demagogues? I suggest their advantage in detecting and exploiting the citizens' anxieties has a very simple explanation. It is that a typical demagogue employs the same *anthropomorphic* notions of a state as the man in the street. Sometimes he sees the state, in anthropomorphic guise, as though it were a personified leader who will solve the citizens' problems and bear their guilts; sometimes he sees it, in no less anthropomorphic guise, as though it were a primitive tribe whose members they are and whose conquests and crimes they share. In fact, they may not only share the crimes, they may also transmit them to their descendants, for the guilts of the tribe are regarded as hereditary. One way or the other, the anthropomorphic notion of a state either transfers the burden to a demagogic leader or imposes it on persons who are really innocent. As long as men continue to think of the state as some sort of human figure, whether natural or allegorical, or some tribal agglomeration, they will remain unready to understand the moral dimensions of democratic citizenship.

The writings of political philosophers being shot through with anthropomorphism, there is no occasion for wonder that these primitive notions still survive and flourish. Aristotle, who had postulated a state so small that one could see all of it at a single view, understandably went on to argue that the good for a state was the same as the good for a man. A state would include many men, but "many" meant only a few thousands to him. Since the citizens of Athens assembled for action as a tribe or union of tribes, it seemed appropriate for him to assess their state decisions according to the same criteria as their individual decisions.

By like token, during the Middle Ages when society had been reorganized on a feudal, hierarchic basis, it seemed plausible for John of Salisbury, England's earliest political theorist, to compare the state to a human body. The prince, he said, was the head; the priests were the soul and presided over the entire body; the senate was the heart; the judges and governors of provinces were the eyes, ears, and tongue; the soldiers were the armed hand; the officials, advocates, and magistrates were the unarmed hand; the prince's attendants were the sides; the fiscal officers were the stomach and intestines; and the husbandmen were the feet, which clung to the soil, supported the body, and needed the care of the head to keep them from stumbling.

The anthropomorphic fallacy went on. In the seventeenth century, a king, claiming to absorb the entire body politic in his own person, declared, "L'état c'est moi." This was the acme of anthropomorphic fiction for a long while, that is, until the next century when the royal title of "sovereign"—which sensible men had long been wont to take as lightly as "your grace" when applied to a duke or "your honor" when applied to a magistrate or "justice" or "peace" when applied to a justice of the peace—this title of "sovereign" was asserted to belong as of right to several million assorted American citizens, at least to those among them who were called "the good people" of the states. Yet, curiously enough, the same theorists who were accustomed to say that the American people were sovereign insisted with like vehemence that the United States Government was sovereign and so too was each of the constituent states. While some few unsophisticated individuals still believed that a "sovereign" should not mean a state but a monarch who ruled over a state, this was charitably ascribed to naïveté or weakness of understanding on their part. Otherwise they would know, as every cartoonist knew, that sovereignty was a term for bespangled and beaming Uncle Sam, for the State of Mississippi in a truculent pose, for the worried British lion with knots in his tail, and for a temporarily thwarted Russian bear. Unfortunately, it is out of such stuff as this that men have fashioned laws and judicial decisions.

If the modern state is not functionally equivalent to a man or a tribe (not to mention a lion, bear, or eagle), is it then to be treated as exempt of moral restraints in its action and administration? How ought one pass judgment on what it does or fails to do? We recognize—or ought to recognize—that a state can rightfully do many things that it would be wrong for a man to do. With complete justice and propriety, it can take our property in taxes, regulate our business affairs, try us in court and incarcerate us, compel us to submit to education, vaccination, and registration, and conscript us to military service. On the other hand, no modern state even claims to be immune to moral standards. None claims a Machiavellian license to disregard all morality and pursue mere naked interest. Certainly, the democratic state cannot. It is neither an ordinary man controlled by a strictly individual morality nor a Renaissance prince controlled by no morality at all. There are moral standards that apply to the state, but we shall not commence to develop them without first understanding why it is that, despite all the cartoons and allegories, a state is not like a man.

To begin with, most people comprehend that a state is not like a man in size or power. Clearly, the difference in size is not a mere matter of geographical expanse, for this might be offset by speed of transportation and communication. The real difference consists rather in the sheer numbers of the citizens, numbers that have passed the hundreds of thousands, the millions, and the tens of millions to teem—beyond imagination—in the hundreds of millions. One cannot cope with quantities of human beings as one copes with quantities of miles.

Contrasted with the resources of a natural person, the overwhelming force available to a state is undeniably impressive. It comprises almost every coercive weapon, beginning at the highest level with the sentimental pressure of patriotism, proceeding more aggressively through various types of economic compulsion, and continuing to the brute plane of fists, clubs, tear gas, prison walls, bullets, and hangmen's ropes. The state has truly redoubtable powers at its call, theoretically more than enough to overcome every kind of delay or obstacle. Yet as we all know, the work of every existing state, even the most absolute, is hourly thwarted in countless ways. Officials may seem to enjoy supreme power but they cannot clear their way of burglars or pickpockets or pimps, sleeping policemen, sclerotic bureaucrats, corrupt administrators, idlers in the public offices, thick-witted oafs in the factories, defiant housewives in the market, or heedless young lovers in the grass. In point of fact, they cannot even monopolize the business of deliberately killing human beings but must share it with jealous husbands, impatient heirs, and professional gangsters.

High officials are often notorious bunglers. There is a story that England lost her American colonies because a minister of state would not postpone a pleasure journey from London to Kent long enough to sign the order which directed Lord Howe to advance up the Hudson Valley and effect a junction with General Burgoyne, marching down from Quebec; and if one finds anything to suspect in the story, it is only the detail that the order had been presented for signature at the office of the right minister. Nevertheless, despite all their limitations and ineptitudes, there is no denying that national states do represent enormous power.

It seems to me that the critical differences between a state and an individual man have less to do with size and power, the physical factors, than with time and function, the biological factors. A human being's moral transactions—at least, most of them—are linked indissolubly with the cycle of his life. He enters into morally significant relations as he is conceived and born, as he is nurtured, disciplined, and educated, as he consorts in friendship, as he lusts and yearns, enters adulthood, business, parenthood, middle age, old age, and the approach to death. He rises, flourishes, and declines; and whether he chooses or not, his moral calculus necessarily involves not only the usual variables of the life stage he happens to occupy at the moment but, in addition, the inevitable and universal constant that continually modifies and ultimately cancels all variables whatever. Death is our only categorical postulate. Whatever beliefs men may have devised to comfort themselves, whatever hopes they may entertain of individual immortality or resurrection, they all face the simple equation between being born and being on the way to die. In this, our morality is bound to be different from a state's, for a state is expected to maintain its existence permanently and indefinitely.

Thomas Jefferson was wise enough to sense that this very attribute of the state, that is, its assumed quality of deathlessness, would pose certain special problems for an aspiring republican society. Throughout his life, the dilemma troubled him. By what title, he asked, could any single generation of a free people assume to bind successor generations to a set of constitutional and legal dispositions? No matter how wise the founding fathers of a nation might have been when they organized its government, the men of the present age always possessed an inalienable right to make their own decisions, rule themselves, and discard outworn institutions. He felt the conviction so strongly that, at the beginning of our government, he proposed that all constitutions, laws, and public debts should expire automatically every nineteen years unless the new generation should deliberately choose to adopt and renew them. Though as a concrete, specific proposal this notion of Jefferson's was quite useless and impractical, there was an important political truth behind it. Jefferson discerned that a state does not conform to the human life cycle; it may renew its youth when a man cannot; it may prosper indefinitely at stages when a man must decline or it may decline and dissolve for causes which would leave a man untouched. Unlike a man's body, the "body politic" cannot be conceived or generated once for all. Its destiny must depend on continual acts of new creation and new revelation.

This insight—that the creating of a state is a continuous and unending process—applies particularly to the variety of functions that a modern state performs. If we should assert in practical terms that a state is whatever it does, then in the light of the history of the past century we should have to conclude that the state is certainly not what it used to be and that it will probably not continue to be what it is, for it performs many functions which we consider indispensable today, though they were left to private hands or simply left undone only a generation ago. There is no possibility of tying the national state down to a fixed list of activities just because we happen to find them familiar in our time. States are continually compelled to grapple with the novel and unfamiliar. Who in the world of political realities could have anticipated that the twentieth century would witness the emergent problems and functions of interplanetary exploration?

In such a time as ours, it seems only reasonable that democratic thinking should graduate from immaturity and discard the crude, outworn anthropomorphic illusions of the past. This would be the first step in developing a philosophy fit for free men.

### *A Consumer Perspective*

Once the step is taken, anyone can see that what we call the state is only an improvised arrangement charged with the performance of certain social functions and manned with certain more or less competent workers. From time to time we change the functions, adding to them rather more often than we subtract, and at fixed intervals we change the staff of official workers, who likewise tend to become more numerous than they used to be. Occasionally, by installing some extensive new activity like social and welfare insurance or by amending the provisions of the constitution, we may alter the basic structure of the arrangement. Meanwhile, we can think of it in a variety of ways. At certain times and for certain purposes, we may choose to conceive of the state as a real and separate entity; at other times and for other purposes, we may prefer to consider it as though it were only an aggregate name for the squads of officials who perform the respective public functions. Either way—whether we are considering it as real or as merely nominal for the purpose at hand—there are various important advantages to be secured by depersonalizing it. The moment we depersonalize the state, we find ourselves better able to personalize the officials, on the one hand, and the general citizenry, on the other, and this is the very beginning of a democratic attitude and a democratic temper.

For there is a certain kind of sentiment or temper that can be associated specifically with democracy. Since no one feels like a democrat every moment of the day, we all slip in and out of the temper. We cast it aside whenever we feel disillusioned and cynical, since it is neither of these, or when we feel mystically exalted or truculently arrogant or humbly servile and abased, since it is certainly none of these. Nor is the democratic temper a mere undifferentiated feeling of patriotism, for there have always been innumerable excellent patriots in countries under autocratic rule. Patriotism, pathetically enough, can be found almost anywhere.

What then is the specifically democratic temper? It is a firm respect for oneself displayed as a sort of briny irreverence toward officials. Democratic irreverence does not ordinarily imply rebellion or even disrespect; its eye-level gaze implies only that the citizen sees the official for what he is, i.e., just another person performing a socially assigned task with more or less competence and ability.

In this relation, the citizen's attitude of irreverence is not truly democratic unless it is actuated by some modicum of respect for his own dignity, character, and judgment. If he happens to believe that all men, including himself and the official he is confronting, are hopelessly sinful, corrupt, stupid, or constrained by deterministic forces, then his temper will be irreverent but not democratic. If he feels that all the governed are worthless and all the governors wise and good, or vice versa, he will likewise lack the democratic temper. For the temper is the emotional equivalent of a bold and audacious assertion. Through affective manner, emotional pitch, and tone of expression, it asserts that democracy has canceled and obliterated the old line of separation between governments and peoples, that democratic citizens are really operative units and elements within the government, that they are among the number of the governors at the same time that they are among the governed, and that the only acceptable distinction between an official and a general citizen is that the official's governmental powers, functions, and duties are more narrowly defined and specialized. In short, the participative citizen in a democracy may feel that he too holds an office—in Aristotle's radiant phrase, an "indefinite office."

The democratic temper does not come with equal force or pervasiveness to every citizen. Sometimes even a highly independent and critical mind may feel the need to reserve some private niche for the practice of reverence. For example, in Alfred North Whitehead's early years when he was obliged to ride about London on a bus, he used to pretend that he took some famous person along for company. They would sit together, usually on the upper deck, and converse heatedly with each other. Whitehead would explain the passing sights and monuments and ask his interlocutor to comment on them. In this way, he often took Sir Isaac Newton along, or Archimedes, or Aristotle. But somehow he never invited Plato, whom he admired most. Though he never explained the reason, it is easy to see that his extreme feeling of reverence and nothing else was what stood between Plato and the pleasure of many interesting bus rides. A charming, even lovable, vagary it was on Whitehead's part, typical of his sweet personality. Yet in the democratic temper things are entirely different, and we sense danger, instead of charm, when men display too much respect for great personages, whether living or dead. No one must be considered too wise or virtuous for an occasional ride atop the democratic bus.

Sometimes, this free and easy democratic temper of ours has rather peculiar methods of expressing itself. If there is no other simple way to personalize a high official and make him intelligible to the citizen-mass, then the press, radio, and television will present his life and condition in physiological terms. If he is healthy at the time, they are at a disadvantage; they can only tell how he takes exercises, controls his girth, eats and drinks, cares for his teeth, plays at various sports, relaxes, and sleeps; but if he happens to fall ill of some really dangerous disease, his path to popular sympathy and understanding is easy. No longer a distant symbol of awesome official power, he becomes familiar and intelligible, a man among other men. Many will sympathize with him out of kindness, others out of satisfied malice. The malicious will no longer begrudge his success and authority, now that he suffers from the same ailment as their bosses or brothers-in-law. They say, Let him enjoy all the limousines and military salutes while we enjoy the doctors' bulletins about the rate of his pulse. If, therefore, high officials must fall ill from time to time, perhaps it is a solace, though a wry one, that their illness enables some wretched onlookers to recognize and feel a common humanity.

A citizen with a healthy psyche does not need morbid occasions like these to assume a democratic temper, for he already knows that government officials are not different from other human beings. They suffer from the same defects, limitations, and shortcomings as other men; their legal power to do greater good or greater ill only precipitates the exposure of their defects and aggravates the results of their shortcomings. And how chance plays with them! Often when they deliberate and propose most reasonably, the ultimate event is entirely unreasonable; and when they move ahead recklessly or foolishly, some fortuitous circumstance intervenes to rescue them. Did they store up grain? The next harvest will prove enormous. Did they empty the warehouses? An unpredictable drought will destroy the crops. When they plan for a multitude, only a few apply, and when they plan for few, the demands are innumerable. When they endeavor to ban a book, their decree may advertise it and save it from oblivion. If they explain official policies in detail, they bore the electorate; if they fail to explain, they may be loudly accused of arrogance and corruption.

These are the regular incidents of political life and discussion even in the older, more experienced democracies. What they amount to is by no means so irrational or contradictory as it may seem. Though the democratic temper is not intended to assist logical dissecting or strict parsing in abstract terms, it does convey a significant set of expectations and demands. It asserts in effect: "For centuries we have argued our human case on any ground or combination of grounds we thought you officials might consider and respect. We have based our claims, at one time or another, on Magna Carta, the Bill of Rights, and a score of other state documents; we have referred you to religious teachings and ethical principles of every sort and origin; we have contended for the customary and traditional rights of Englishmen, Americans, and many other peoples; we have deduced arguments from the just purposes of a lawful government and the sources of its just powers; we have drawn inferences from a creed of popular sovereignty; and we have continually insisted on what men call their 'natural and inalienable' rights. Our bitter experiences with official behavior in every age and country have taught us to cling to all of these contentions—whether they be tenable or obsolete, consistent or mutually contradictory—and we renounce none of them. At the same time, we now possess a new title to freedom and justice, the outcome and corollary of our modern representative democracy. This new title you will scarcely be able to refute, for we rely henceforth not only on an assertion of our rights but also on an empirical demonstration of your incompetences, *the functional incompetences of officials.*"

Taken by itself, the democratic temper might have an almost anarchic effect and might inspire a blind, indiscriminate recalcitrance to the whole business of being governed. Sometimes when the mood of a people becomes tired, bored, and perverse, the temper will find expression in crudely rejecting whoever happens to be in office, casting him out only because he is in, and elevating someone else for no better reason than the prospect of hearing a new name and seeing a new face. Republics, it has been said, are lamentably ungrateful to their chosen leaders, even as ungrateful on occasion as emperors, kings, and other despots. But often what appears like ingratitude in a republic is not that at all but only a sudden, surging popular insistence on the adoption of a "consumer perspective." When the democratic temper expresses itself constructively, it impels men to look at government and law in a consumer perspective.

This is no automatic or easy accomplishment, since it opposes the fixed and habitual attitudes of virtually all past eras. The old political, social, and legal perspective, developed and reinforced over millennia of time and continents of space, was determined by the dominant interests of rulers, governors, and other officers; it was strictly imperial or official. The classic philosophers of government, at least after the death of Aristotle, developed their theories while observing the ways of empires, kingdoms, landed aristocracies, or oligarchies. Consequently, to achieve a consumer perspective a shift of as much as 180 degrees is called for.

Whenever a concrete question arises for decision within a given society, most of the inhabitants recognize the same factors as relevant to resolving it and, if they disagree on the answer, it is only because they see the factors in different ratios of size, consequence, and importance. Almost everything in the process of deliberation depends on where they take their stand while they assess them, on what we correctly call their "point of view." Even in the old imperial or official perspective, if a ruler happens to be extraordinarily intelligent, he may reason that the welfare of the people conduces to the strength of the state and that conscientious administration of justice promotes solidarity and patriotism; he may go so far as to perceive that freedom of opinion furnishes a safety valve for grievances and discontents. And even in the new consumer perspective, if citizens happen to believe that particular political, economic, or social circumstances require it, they may reason that the strength of the state is a prime condition of the people's welfare, that the administrative efficiency of the officials is important enough to justify inconvenience, expense, or sacrifice on the part of the community, and that, in an extreme posture of affairs, good citizens will restrain their political criticisms and swallow their grievances. It is not this or that factor that is new or different in the consumer perspective but the relative consequence to be accorded to the several factors when the hour comes for judgment.

How does a person become a consumer of government and law? The obvious and traditional way consists in being safeguarded and regulated from day to day as he goes about the chores of his life and fills his place in society; in this sense, he consumes law whenever he buys or sells, rents or rides, pays or receives. In addition, there is a more dramatic way to consume the law: one may engage in a lawsuit, for example, or be charged with a crime, like the unfortunate young man we have met, named Joe. These are the passive manners of consuming.

Under democratic government, a citizen also consumes government and law actively. He influences the shape of policy and law, casts his vote, supports his political party, urges reforms, organizes and asserts the interests of a special group.

Finally, there is a third way to consume government, the way we have already identified as our new moral condition. It consists in examining, judging, and assuming responsibility for what our representatives do in our name and by our authority, the unjust and evil acts as well as the beneficent and good.

Here is where the consumer perspective becomes decisive. If anyone attempts to quiet our misgivings by insisting—as many a respectable lawyer will—that unlawful police methods, official brutalities, and corrupt cases such as Joe's are unimportant because they do not happen often (or are not often exposed, which is all he can truthfully claim), we may be quite certain that he is advocating the old, callous perspective of predemocratic days. In the view of things he is assuming, outrages and injustices look like mere statistical blunders—regrettable as all blunders are and the more regrettable because, by becoming too numerous, they may eventually impair the general efficacy of government administration. Meanwhile, as far as he is concerned, certain prosecutors can continue to slumber by night and certain judges by day.

Only when we put the old view aside and adopt a consumer perspective are we able to perceive the practical significance of our institutions, laws, and public transactions in terms of their impacts on the lives and homely experiences of human beings. It is these personal impacts that constitute the criteria for any appraisal we may make. How, we ask, does the particular institution affect personal rights and personal concerns, the interests and aspirations of individual, group, and community? We judge it according to its concussions on human lives.

Adopting a consumer perspective does not involve favoring unregulated private enterprise, obsolete economic individualism or, for that matter, any uniform system of property tenure. Nor is the perspective just one more futile philosophic effort either to isolate the individual person from his social and economic context or to submerge him in it, to establish him at some fixed place in a hierarchy of values or to give him or the community priority one over the other. Rather is it a point from which to assess representative officials for what they ought to be—not Caesars or envoys of Caesars but fellow governors exercising highly specialized functions, and no better equipped than others, except in various technical aspects, to speak for the general community and its welfare.

According to the old imperial or official perspective, it would be warrantable though deeply regrettable that a man be put to death unjustly in order to preserve the order, dignity, and tranquillity of the state; according to the consumer perspective, a state preservable only at such a cost would not be worth preserving. The choice of perspective makes a decisive practical difference.

On the current American scene the old imperial perspective, obsolete as it is, still controls the thinking of most lawyers, judges, politicians, and businessmen; it still determines the outcome of momentous public issues. For example, recently a man by the name of

Alfonse Bartkus came before the United States Supreme Court to claim that he had been unconstitutionally tried twice for the same alleged crime. He had gone through a complete trial in a federal court on a charge of robbing a federally insured savings and loan association, and the jury had acquitted him. Thereupon, the United States authorities had assisted the district attorney of the State of Illinois to prosecute and try him again, in an Illinois court, for the selfsame robbery, and this time the jury had found him guilty. The federal Bill of Rights provides that no person "shall . . . be subject for the same offence to be twice put in jeopardy of life or limb," and all of the Supreme Court judges, conservative and liberal alike, agree that this provision is binding on the State of Illinois, at least when a second prosecution would be "repugnant to the conscience of mankind."

In Bartkus' case, the majority of the Court (5 to 4) held that the second prosecution was entirely constitutional. Since the United States was one "sovereign" and the State of Illinois another and different one, they saw nothing repugnant to the conscience of mankind in having each "sovereign" enforce its own interest by prosecuting Bartkus for the same act. The result seems entirely reasonable if one adopts the old official or imperial perspective.

Justice Hugo L. Black, dissenting, expressed a more complimentary opinion of his country's conscience. Bluntly he urged the Court to adopt a consumer perspective by examining the predicament "from the standpoint of the individual who is being prosecuted." Joined by Chief Justice Warren and Justice Douglas, the great libertarian judge said:

> The Court apparently takes the position that a second trial for the same act is somehow less offensive if one of the trials is conducted by the Federal Government and the other by a State. Looked at from the standpoint of the individual who is being prosecuted, this notion is too subtle for me to grasp. If double punishment is what is feared, it hurts no less for two "Sovereigns" to inflict it than for one. If danger to the innocent is emphasized, that danger is surely no less when the power of State and Federal Governments is brought to bear on one man in two trials, than

when one of these "Sovereigns" proceeds alone. In each case, inescapably, a man is forced to face danger twice for the same conduct.

To understand the full influence of the old imperial perspective on the majority of the judges, one need only consider that the prohibition of "double jeopardy" can be traced back through medieval to Greek and Roman times, that it appears in nearly every formal compact and declaration of rights in American history, and that the enormously enhanced powers and functions of modern officials and bureaucrats make it more essential now than in any previous era. The Bartkus decision is unhappily a representative one, for despite smatterings of progress, no single field of American law or operation of the government reflects a consumer perspective thoroughly or wholeheartedly. After all the past generations of social criticism and reform, human beings continue to get tangled in a skein of obsolete legal abstractions while more fortunate fellow citizens sit patiently by, observe the disasters, and cluck their regrets. Meanwhile, disturbing though it be for us to recall the circumstance, it was in the purported name of *all* the people of Illinois, and with the purported constitutional permission of *all* the people of the United States, that Alfonse Bartkus was prosecuted again and convicted after his acquittal.

### *The Given and the Created*

It is generally accepted nowadays that the objectives of a society shift, evolve, and mutate over a period of time. Ideas have histories, currents, and careers of their own, and a political maxim or standard can gradually come to convey a whole register of different meanings as new cultural circumstances emerge. This much is familiar to the literature of political philosophy. What the philosophers have tended to neglect—perhaps because they desired to disregard local details in order to generalize more freely, perhaps because their sophistication in semantics led them to disesteem mere writings, perhaps because they were too entranced with history as flowing reason and cascading purpose to notice the boulders and tree trunks that occasionally fill the stream and deflect the current—at any rate, philosophers have undervalued the causal role of positive, recorded facts, formal documents, and hard historical events.

Though they do indeed make it more difficult for one to generalize, the hard facts of the past are incontrovertibly there—and, what is more important, many of them are still operative, still present among us here. The historical Given, which, of course, includes what we may call "the documentary Given," simply refuses to be banished from a tenable political philosophy. The Given makes a working difference. It makes a difference of substance and moment in human affairs that King John did issue the Magna Carta, that William and Mary did assent to the Settlement Act, and that the American people did adopt a written Bill of Rights with just these particular provisions and no others. Similarly, the Declaration of the Rights of Man and of the Citizen is a tough, existential fact of abiding relevance to civil liberties in France. Judges and other officials are confronted not with loose abstractions but with specific texts, containing just such words, provisions, and inhibitions; citizens are endowed with these and no other public promises around which they can rally.

Often the mere existence of a solemn written text prevents a potential political or legal issue from arising or becoming acute. Granted that texts may be worth nothing, or less than nothing, unless they enlist some measure of community support and official implementation; granted that high-sounding guarantees have been proved illusory if not hypocritical on a thousand different occasions: nevertheless, "the documentary Given" deserves almost always to be taken into account. For—whether the country we are concerned with employs one institutional mechanism or another to enforce its traditional ideals, a parliamentary question hour as in Britain or a high court as in the United States—the mere availability of a time-honored text often has immediate practical consequences. The grave evocation of an inherited maxim can give pause to one kind of official action and support to another kind, discountenance one public attitude and confer prestige on another, instill self-reproach in one individual and enable another, by retracing the ancient aspirations of his people, to confer life and vigor on them. The Given works living changes in the course of politics and history. What, for example, would have been the role of the United States Supreme Court in defending civil rights and liberties if the nation had not adopted a written Constitution and written Bill of Rights, each of which was opposed by some of the ablest minds of the founding age? Without a formal text to rely on, would the judges have assumed to nullify anything that the people's elected representatives might have chosen to do? By like token, without the text of England's Habeas Corpus Act of 1679, innumerable men in every quarter of the globe would not have been set free but would have lingered and died in a variety of illegal confinements.

Valuable though a particular national document may be, since it too belongs to the living, it ought not be read in the fading light of its origins but rather in the high noon of the present situation. We do not honor a useful inherited text when we proceed to commit the genetic fallacy with its meaning. On the contrary, a text deserves to rank as a constitution only insofar as we rescue it from the past and use it to grapple with the problems of the present and the conceived future.

Moreover, it is worth remarking that noble content and fine rhetoric alone do not make a political text important. In point of fact, there are narrow limits to what even the most gifted draftsman can contribute to the eventual career and destiny of his document. These are for others to decide at a later time. The draftsman is rather like an archer who wanders about in a forest and tests the quality of his bow by shooting his shafts at various knots in the trees. Many years later, some idle boy who has come upon a bucket of paint amuses himself by drawing circles of different sizes around a few of the embedded arrows. In time most of the arrows fall to the ground, most of the circles fade away. Finally, other men arrive on the scene, discover a painted circle on a tree with an arrow directly in its center, and exclaim, "A bull's-eye!"

One of these historic bull's-eyes—assuredly a bull's-eye for the conditions of our present era—was scored by a certain provision of the English Bill of Rights of 1689. Reacting against the prison tortures and lingering deaths which had disgraced the reigns of Restoration Stuarts, the English Parliament, with the assent of William and Mary, resolved that never again should "cruel and unusual punishments" be inflicted. This prohibition, which may be traced in principle at least as far back as Magna Carta, was adopted literally in the American Bill of Rights. Here the clause lay somnolent throughout the nineteenth century, the Supreme Court using it merely to hold that there was nothing unconstitutional about inflicting capital punishment by a firing squad or an electric chair instead of the traditional noose. Then, early in the twentieth century, the whole problem of "cruel and unusual punishments" launched on an adventurous new career, replete with challenge and conflict. The successive episodes in the Supreme Court make a working specimen of democratic creation and revelation. They display the judges in the very process of creating new social values—not, however, as the legend says God created the firmament and the world, *ex nihilo*, but rather as God created man, out of soil that was already created and waiting to be used.

The text says solemnly that the government will inflict no "cruel and unusual punishments." But what ought one take for the meaning in a concrete case? What ought the United States, speaking through its supreme tribunal, declare to be prohibited as "cruel and unusual"? There have been three momentous decisions to mark the route toward an answer.

The first case came before the Court in 1910, that is, during the period when the United States was holding the Philippine Islands, taken from Spain in the Spanish-American War, and preparing them for self-government and national independence. Paul Weems, a Coast Guard disbursing officer, had been convicted of making false entries amounting to 616 pesos in a cashbook of the Philippine Lighthouse Service and had been sentenced to fifteen years of "Cadena with accessories" and a substantial fine. The "Cadena with accessories" was a punishment inherited from the centuries of Spanish dominion. Under it, Weems would carry a chain night and day attached to his ankles and wrists, would be employed at hard and painful labor, would be cut off from all civil, political, and family connections, and would, after serving the term and for the rest of his life, be kept under continual surveillance so that he could not even change his domicile without the permission of a magistrate. Was this punishment "cruel and unusual"?

Two of our justices, White and Holmes, insisted it was not, at least in any constitutional sense. According to their view, no punishment was prohibited or intended to be prohibited by the Bill of Rights unless it was of the same nature as the cruel bodily tortures used in England before 1689. In all other respects, anything the local legislature might approve as a method of punishment was permissible and could not be considered "cruel and unusual."

But four justices (three of the nine did not sit on the case) held otherwise, and Weems prevailed. The "cruel and unusual" clause did not merely prohibit the evil practices of the Stuarts; it reached any device that would inflict an excessive, degrading, or inhuman penalty. As for the purposes of the Founding Fathers, it seemed only fair to infer that they too would approve the Court's conferring an ongoing and ambulatory interpretation on their words. Repeatedly they had shown their hostility to unlimited power in anyone's hands, even in the hands of a popular legislature. "In the application of a constitution, therefore, our contemplation cannot be only of what has been but of what may be." The American Bill of Rights forbade imposition of the "Cadena."

Our contemplation, the justices said, should extend to "what may be"—words which were to prove prophetic beyond the possible dreams and nightmares of any sane person living in a civilized society of 1910. At that time, it was impossible that anyone could have foreseen the wholesale and retail cruelties which Mussolini and Stalin would introduce in their countries, the new refinements and subtle ingenuities of mental and physical torture, the mass slave labor and concentration camps, or Hitler's systematic elevation of sadism to an exact science and regular institute of government. What, indeed, may *not* be?

But the holding in Weems' case, we must admit, was merely a fortuitous departure for the new career of the "cruel and unusual" clause. In it, the four judges of the majority were able to profit from a dual advantage. For one thing, the "Cadena," being originally a Spanish device, came into court burdened with a variety of Anglo-American biases. There was a deep though unexpressed association with what one had read about the Spanish Inquisition and there was also a more or less natural distrust of methods unfamiliar and exotic. For another thing, the judges were free to save Weems without insulting any American legislature by labeling its law as "cruel." Even the Philippine legislators would not need to take umbrage, for they had simply left the old Spanish law unchanged on their books.

An authentic test of the Court's courage would come only when it might have to face some systematic and deliberate penal policy of an American legislature. An American form of punishment would be neither unfamiliar nor exotic; it would come into court with the sanction and prestige of popularly elected representatives; and presumably it could not be called "cruel" without reflecting in some way on its authors. What government, indeed, ever admits it is being cruel presently, i.e., now and in this immediately impending act? Very occasionally a government may concede that, in a time clearly past and under a repudiated regime, it has inflicted some cruelty or other. But can one ask it to concede present cruelty, and this in a democracy, which supposedly derives the standards of its laws from the moral attitudes of the people?

In the second important case, the Court was again presented with a boon of fortune. A Negro by the name of Willie Francis having committed murder, the State of Louisiana had sentenced him to death by electrocution. He was placed in the electric chair and the current was turned on. It passed through his body but did not kill him. Then he petitioned the Supreme Court to forbid a second official attempt at electrocution on the ground that it would be "cruel and unusual." Since no similar case had arisen or was likely to arise thereafter, the judges had an extraordinarily fortunate opportunity to prevent the cruelty without affronting the moral standards of a popular legislature. What had been exotic in Paul Weems' case was more than paralleled by what was "unusual" and fortuitous in Willie Francis'. The blame for diminishing the punishment could be laid at the door of mere chance, which is accustomed to receiving such foundlings and never tries to return them. Thus the case offered an unusual opportunity.

By a vote of five to four, the Court failed its opportunity and permitted the State of Louisiana to proceed with a second electrocution. There were three different lines of reasoning.

Four judges said they could see nothing "cruel" in a second electrocution because the situation was due only to an accidental, mechanical breakdown and the state authorities had not intended and did not intend to be cruel. Their view provides a historic instance of the imperial or official perspective in action. According to them, government is to be considered cruel in the pains it inflicts only when it intends to employ cruelty; cruelty felt, experienced, and suffered is immaterial. One can scarcely read this curious show of logic without recalling the ancient comment of Bion that, though boys throw stones at frogs in sport, yet the frogs do not die in sport but in earnest.

Four other judges expressed a deep revulsion against the proposed second execution, which would surely be cruel and unusual. They said: "Lack of intent that the first application be less than fatal is not material. The intent of the executioner cannot lessen the torture or excuse the result." Here is the consumer perspective in its full clarity and humanity. "Cruel" is a term to communicate certain experiences of the consumers of law. Cruel is what cruel does, what functions cruelly. If we conceive that an average consumer—not the extremely callous, not the hypersensitive, not the masochistic either —would find the punishment not merely unwelcome and painful but actually cruel, then it must be cruel, whatever the officials may have intended.

In a separate opinion, speaking only for himself, Justice Frankfurter gave the decisive vote which resolved the tie and permitted a second execution. His line of analysis was disconcerting to a degree. While protesting a "personal feeling of revulsion" against the second execution, he could find no reason to attribute a comparable moral reaction to the American people, whose consensus and conscience supplied the legal standard for his judgment. Accordingly, Willie Francis was subjected to a second—and "successful"—electrocution. Rarely, I believe, has the conscience of a great people been esteemed so low by one whom they had deputed to administer their highest interest, which consists in public justice.

It is interesting that, in each of the cases we have rehearsed, no more than four justices could be marshaled to animate the "cruel and unusual" clause. Strikingly enough, the same thing occurred in the case of Albert Trop, which was the third momentous decision. But in Trop's case, an independent concurring opinion furnished the fifth vote and gave a majority to the consumer position. Justice Frankfurter now became the active spokesman of the dissenters.

In Trop's case, as we shall see, there was nothing either exotic or accidental to ease the burden of the Court. To make matters more difficult, the punishment which Trop was contesting had been prescribed, not by one of the fifty states but by the federal Congress, which had assumed to legislate on the subject under its constitutional war powers, acting at the request of the President, who is constitutional commander in chief. If ever the enforcement of "cruel and unusual" would require courage on the high bench, this was the instance.

In 1944, during World War II, Trop, a native of Ohio, twenty years of age and a private in the United States Army, was serving in French Morocco. On May 22nd he escaped from a stockade where he had been confined for breach of discipline. He returned voluntarily the next day, explaining that he was getting cold and hungry. A court-martial convicted him of desertion and sentenced him to three years at hard labor, forfeiture of all pay and allowances, and a dishonorable discharge. The sentence was enforced.

In 1952 Trop applied for a passport. It was denied because the Nationality Act of 1940 provided that he had lost his American citizenship by being convicted and dishonorably discharged for wartime desertion. Trop appealed to the Supreme Court, claiming that to denationalize him would be a "cruel and unusual punishment."

With characteristic brilliance, Justice Frankfurter presented the dissenters' view of the case as it appeared in an imperial or official perspective. The Act providing for Trop's denationalization, he submitted, could not be said to impose "cruel and unusual punishment" because it did not impose "punishment" at all; it was only a measure for regulating the armed forces and maintaining their discipline. The Cabinet Committee who had prepared the statute had expressly called it "nonpenal." How then could a court treat the Act as inflicting "punishment"? And even assuming it did, Justice Frankfurter added, surely to denationalize Trop could not be considered "cruel" in view of the fact that wartime desertion had always been considered a capital offense. "Is constitutional dialectic so empty of reason," he demanded, "that it can be seriously urged that loss of citizenship is a fate worse than death?" In all, his was a strong and coherent opinion, revealing how very much depends on the perspective one begins by adopting.

It was Chief Justice Earl Warren who delivered the prevailing judicial opinion. He remarked that what a Cabinet Committee might have said about the law could scarcely bind the Court or determine the case. "How simple would be the tasks of constitutional adjudication and of law generally if specific problems could be solved by inspection of the labels pasted on them!" Despite the committee's characterization, the law was penal in substance because its purposes and effects were manifestly punitive. "Punishment" it clearly was; the crucial question was whether it was "cruel." In deciding this question, the traditional use of the death penalty for desertion furnished no index; it gave the government no license to torture a man or consign him to an uncivilized fate. For if one examines the practical impacts on a human being, what is this proposed punishment of denationalization?

It is a form of punishment more primitive than torture, for it destroys for the individual the political existence that was centuries in the development. The punishment strips the citizen of his status in the national and international political community. His very existence is at the sufferance of the country in which he happens to find himself. While any one country may accord him some rights, and presumably as long as he remained in this country he would enjoy the limited rights of an alien, no country need do so because he is stateless. Furthermore, his enjoyment of even the limited rights of an alien might be subject to termination at any time by reason of deportation. In short, the expatriate has lost the right to have rights. . . .

The civilized nations of the world are in virtual unanimity that statelessness is not to be imposed as punishment for crime. . . . The United Nations' survey of the nationality laws of 84 nations of the world reveals that only two countries, the Philippines and Turkey, impose denationalization as a penalty for desertion. In this country the Eighth Amendment forbids this to be done.

Here we have a working model of the consumer perspective, complemented and perfected by a comparison with the practices of other nations, or what Thomas Jefferson would have called "a decent respect to the opinion of mankind." The comparison with foreign practices is indispensable; as any intelligent patriot realizes, no country can aspire to teach in the universal seminar of moral standards unless it endeavors simultaneously to learn something there. No country can be justified in preening itself or displaying complacency, for the forward steps it takes are characteristically tardy, insufficient, and—as we have seen—precarious. Yet we know that they can be genuine and true. . . .

In this chapter, we have been describing the background of our moral involvement. We have been marking certain major drives in the democratic thought of our times: first, the drive to discard an anthropomorphic notion of sovereignty; second, the drive to develop a consumer perspective; and third, the drive to use the past, the traditional, and the Given as material for new progress and creation. Now we are ready to confront our main predicament as citizens of a free and representative government. We can begin by asking whether the mere status of being a citizen makes one automatically responsible for official wrongs.

# II

# *Defining the Vicarious Responsibilities*

# III

# *Citizenship: Collective Responsibilities*

## *The Restatement of Responsibility*

For an inquiry such as ours, there are special advantages in starting from the case of Tillie's son Joe who was falsely convicted of robbery and murder. Cases like Joe's are not only typical of what oppression means in any time, culture, or legal system; they have the additional feature—which makes them the more representative for our purposes—of arising under laws which undoubtedly belong on a civilized statute book. Inasmuch as all reasonable persons, including Tillie and Joe, approve the existence of laws against robbery and homicide, none of us would feel impelled to oppose this particular prosecution unless and until we learned the secret of its corruptness. None need feel that the moral position was similar to, say, a prosecution under a racial-segregation ordinance, where the nature of the statute itself would give us notice that wrong was being done under the guise of law. In Joe's case, if we are to be implicated, it must be as mere electors and in no other capacity. And since no one—no matter how high his qualifications in a specialized field, no matter how much he may know about courts, police, education and juvenile delinquency, about ethics and religion, about business and taxes, about science and technology, or about medicine and surgery—since no one can aspire to a level of absolute and universal expertness, every single one of us is usually bound to play the role of a mere elector.

As every citizen has a rather obvious incentive to clarify the extent of his own responsibility for the wrongful acts of officials, it may seem curious that the problem of definition has remained almost precisely where it was at the beginning of the republican era. But this static condition is not really curious at all, certainly not in any innocuous sense; properly understood, it is rather sinister, because it symptomizes a more or less conscious strategy of evasion and confusion in democratic political thinking. And—as the Romans were wont to inquire—for whose benefit? For the unmistakable benefit of the imperial or official perspective and its spokesmen.

As long as citizens can be kept in a state of vicarious involvement that is vague and indefinite, they may remain anxious, uncertain, self-doubtful, and proportionately tame. Perhaps their misgivings will lead them to politicalize the hoary religious doctrine that human beings live under a burden of aboriginal, inherited, and all-pervasive guilt. Perhaps they can be made to believe that all forms of political government—even the democratic forms—are visited on men for their sins and are essentially no more than cores of moral infection from which a virtuous person will hold himself as aloof as possible. They can be reminded that John of Salisbury likened the mass of citizens to the feet of a body politic; and who are the feet that they should assume to question the judgments of the head? In point of fact, it might often be advantageous to the feet that they be protected from knowing just where the head has been leading them. Moreover, if the scope of their involvement is left entirely vague, they may become astute enough to avoid prying into official business. Why, after all, should they inquire and probe if they believe they are obliged to share the very guilts they may disclose? On such considerations, a wise citizenry may be induced to pursue their private business and leave the public business to officials. At least, this is the way citizens have frequently reasoned and officials have frequently profited.

For us it seems high time to adopt an entirely different perspective —our own perspective as consumers of democratic government— and define the true limits of our electoral responsibilities. In the consumer perspective, we do not see democratic government as given men for their sins or as a collective criminal conspiracy which would convert them into principals or moral accessories whenever an official happens to commit an evil act. We do not regard our political compact as some species of collective covenant for the execution of crimes and wrongs, making each and all of us equally guilty along with the official perpetrators. Since it was for justice, equality, and liberty that we covenanted with one another, we see no reason to acknowledge a universal burden of vicarious guilts. Whatever despotisms may do, a democratic government cannot be converted into a criminal conspiracy—unless, that is, the officials chance to become so hopelessly corrupt that there is no remaining segment of decency. As long as decency can enlist even a small company of honest defenders—they would correspond to the minimum of ten righteous men who, if the Lord could have found them in the city, would have induced Him to spare Sodom from destruction—representative government does not have the moral implications of a collective cabal. Nor are the electors automatic moral accessories to official crimes. In Joe's case, the evil acts committed by the district attorney and police did not pollute the citizens with moral guilt.

This is not to say, however, that there is no electoral responsibility at all in the circumstances. We have been considering Joe's case strictly in terms of vicarious *guilt*—that is, in terms analogous to what the law would call "criminal." But guilt is by no means equivalent to the whole of moral responsibility, nor is it the only possible form of moral involvement. It is possible for the citizens to become involved collectively without receiving a stain of guilt. For example, one may find, without imputation of guilt, that the electors have incurred the moral equivalent of a "civil" duty or obligation and that, if they fail to discharge it, they will be morally in *default.* Here it is that the real pattern of implication begins to emerge and become precise for us. Although, in short, the electors are not to be considered as participating in an official crime, a subsequent public disclosure of the crime may impose a collective obligation on them to do something about it. The *guilt* attaches to the official perpetrators; if, however, the electors' own obligation is not duly performed, then the responsibility for *default* will attach to them.

It is no wonder that the distinction between the two positions has been clouded from view. Before the advent of the republican era, men were wont to refer to officials as the king's "servants" or "agents," and no one attempted to impute their misconduct to him, because it was axiomatic that the king could do no wrong. Later, when republicans like Jefferson and Madison referred to government officials as the people's "servants" or "agents," they merely intended to keep the officials in a psychologically subordinate posture and remind them of their responsibility to the electorate. For our purposes, the usage is misleading, for it seems to imply that if officials are "agents," electors are invariably principals and must answer for all deeds and misdeeds in the course of the employment.

Yet, except in instances of a popular referendum or some other direct vote on a very specific issue, there is no genuine parallel between political representation and legal agency. To substitute one set of relations for the other is fallacious. Within the limits imposed by decency and fair play, a public official of consequence (for example, a president, congressman, judge, or district attorney) is entitled and obliged to use his own best judgment and do what he concludes congruous with the public interest. As long as he retains his office, he is free to exercise its authority independently. We expect: a legislator to withstand a hysterical and misguided popular clamor; a judge to disregard the legislative prejudgments which we call "bills of attainder"; a president to heed the sober tones of the past and the future when the voice of the present sounds unwisely shrill. Unlike servants and agents, they are required under appropriate circumstances to gainsay us, at least provisionally.

Nor would we have it otherwise. Desiring them to act with independence, we have generally forbidden them to remit their duty of judgment back to their constituents. Except for a few limited referendum provisions in some of our state constitutions, the legislators are not permitted to abdicate their authority to the electorate. If, for example, a law should be passed with a proviso that it would go into effect only if it should be approved at the next popular election, the courts would hold such a law unconstitutional. An "agent" may turn to his principal, ask for instructions, and apply them with safety; but legislators, judges, and executives are obliged to make their own choices and abide by the consequences. As we will not let them think for us, we will not undertake to do their thinking for them.

If, then, the officials are not really our agents, what do we mean when we speak of electoral responsibility? In the consumer perspective that we have adopted, "responsibility" acquires a new meaning. It ceases to describe merely the objective infection of guilt or the subjective feeling of vague anxiety. No longer a static condition of any kind, it becomes for our enterprise an active human process, an itemized social *agenda,* a methodical program for overt behavior. It will emphasize action. Taken in the objective sense, responsibility will express the doing of certain purposeful acts, collective or individual; taken in the subjective sense, it will express the making of rational plans and the resolving to begin executing them at once. In short, when citizens are truly responsible as consumers of law, they have little room for remorse, self-accusation, or fretful penitence because they are too deeply involved in performing a community agenda which they implement by making use of the state and its legal machinery. They are too busy acting out responsibility in the form of prevention, reparation, and protest.

These three—prevention, reparation, and protest—are the living processes of citizenship responsibility, the tools and techniques by which responsibility expresses itself and builds the outlets for its own discharge. It is through them that the concept derives its force and practical meaning. They define the moral burden that electors must bear in a representative system and, by dint of defining the burden, they make it tolerable.

If we were to compare these three great processes, each with the others, it would be difficult to say which of them contributed most toward producing a good society. I suppose that, of the three, prevention would be the obvious choice for preeminence. Certainly, from time immemorial the classic texts of religion and ethics have preached the desirability of prevention, and folk wisdom has openly preferred an ounce of it to a pound of cure. A policy of prevention may reflect a proper solicitude for the welfare of one's neighbors; hence its influence can be benevolent and solidary. Moreover, it proceeds on the belief that through inquiry, deliberation, and rational planning men are able to control their environments at least in part, that by taking thought to themselves they can add to their stature, and that they can employ science, technology, and empirical wisdom in the service of human happiness. Prevention precludes its two rivals, for whenever it really succeeds, there will be no incident of harm or injustice, hence no role for reparation or protest to perform.

To make the case for prevention complete, I must add that certain species of injustice are inherently beyond the reach of reparation. They simply cannot be compensated, and unless they are prevented, the injury must remain perpetual and irreversible. First, there are the types of injury represented by capital punishment and imposed sexual sterilization, which are, by nature, irreversible and irreparable. Then, there are the types represented by discrimination against human beings on racial and religious grounds. These too have to be dealt with in terms of prevention, if only because it is almost impossible to repair them by compensation. It is impossible not only because the psychic damages which discrimination inflicts are likely to be ineradicable but also because a society cannot rationally repair an old set of inequalities by installing a new and inverse set of inequalities. If a particular racial group has been oppressed and maltreated, the society ought to mitigate the controllable symptoms of damage as much as possible, but it cannot hope to reverse the direction of social causation or disregard the effects of history. Since, generally speaking, there is no effective way to compensate for the harms men suffer from unequal treatment, prevention is usually the sole available course and always the best one.

Reparation too has its claim. Anyone who consults the lessons of experience knows that reparation is indispensable to society because prevention so often fails to perform its promise. Grandiose social and economic predictions and the preventive programs which men have built on them have proved false again and again at enormous human cost. Too frequently, it has been the enterprise of so-called prevention that aggravated the damage and necessitated the granting of reparation. Reparation may aver that it is in fact more rational than any scheme of prevention since it relies not on airy expectations of the future but on the concrete, demonstrated experience of the past. Reparation comes to work when the need is not merely contingent or speculative but mature, definite, and manifest.

True, reparation is customarily made in the form of money, which everyone will grant cannot salve every kind of wound and injury. But money has never been the only medium of public or private reparation, and in recent times its role has tended to shrink as jurists have invented other, more appropriate devices. For example, under modern legislation, if a worker is discharged wrongfully, he may be restored not only to his job but also to his seniority status; if a newspaper prints a defamatory statement, it may be required to publish an equally conspicuous retraction. Reparation ought not be identified with the contemptuous proffer of a sum of money.

What would be fitting reparation in a case of unjust imprisonment like Joe's? I suggest Joe would not object to our beginning with the item of money, not only because he can make such ready use of it but also because—in a society like ours—the disbursement of money will lend a tone of sincerity to any other steps we may desire to take. Without a payment of money, our talk of regretting and sympathizing would probably sound hypocritical even to our own ears. When we reimburse him for his economic loss and psychic injury, let us remember to add a reasonable amount for attorneys' fees. A fair-minded society will not only provide and pay independent counsel to defend all indigent persons who are arrested on serious charges; it will also pay the necessary and reasonable defense costs of all accused persons, whatever their economic condition, who are eventually found to be not guilty. As matters now stand in the United States and most other democratic countries, the state, by recognizing no duty of reimbursement after an acquittal, can compel an innocent man to choose between unjust conviction and personal bankruptcy.

What next ought we do? It seems that genuine reparation to one who has suffered as Joe has would have to go much further. It would involve our trying to comprehend Joe's predicament by projecting ourselves into the transaction as it happened and enacting the central roles, particularly the prosecutor's and Joe's. It would involve a public mitigation of Joe's suffering—through official apologies and assistance in the beginning of a new career. The assistance might have to include psychic rehabilitation to enable Joe to return fittingly to the normal pursuits of daily life outside penitentiary walls. It might have to include special efforts at reconciliation through which Joe might be induced to forgive the community and disregard his wrong, though he could not wholly forget it.

Above all, Joe should receive a solemn assurance that his fellow citizens would try to prevent the occurrence of similar outrages, for only this would give him reason to hope that his suffering had not been futile. Reparation is never quite complete unless it can gather part of its meaning in the future; the law uses it habitually as an effective means for prevention or at least discouragement of future wrongdoing. It works forward as well as backward. Consequently, reparation can claim that it surpasses prevention by actually embracing and including it.

Finally, there is the claim of protest which, following the other contestants, prevention and reparation, may seem comparatively poor. Prevention and reparation generally have the assembled police and military powers of the whole state to give them force, while protest rises lonesomely in a private citizen's breast and directs nothing more impressive than the air of that breast which it pushes upward over the larynx. Especially if one looks at the three contestants in an imperial or official perspective, protest appears almost ludicrously weak; it has only a puff of breath to summon.

Yet its claim deserves to be stated. For is not protest the main theme of our earthly existence, from the newborn baby's first resentful wail to the last sigh we exhale on the deathbed? Protest is the motif of our most serious endeavors. What is government but an organized and systematized protest against the tohu-bohu of general violence? What is religion but a protest against abandonment and sin, education but a protest against ignorance, art but a protest against meaninglessness, law but a protest against injustice? For that matter, we are told that God himself performed the supreme gesture of protest when He created the beginning of all beginnings. The entire world lives and aspires in an infinitude of protests against whatever-it-is-that-is.

You say that protest is feeble? Though it may be permissible to disregard its ancient exemplars such as the Hebrew prophets, Socrates, and Jesus, surely no one can fail to notice its thrust and power in the history of every modern nation. Even the autocracies have felt it continually, and how much more the representative democracies! England's political history since Tudor times can be recounted in a chain of solemn protests, some pronounced by Parliament against the Crown, some pronounced by Parliament against the colonists, some pronounced by others against Parliament.

American independence was no sooner established on the basis of a long series of protests against the English government than Jefferson and Madison launched eloquent protests against their own government in the Virginia and Kentucky Resolutions of 1798. When Jefferson became President and Madison Secretary of State, Chief Justice John Marshall protested against their behavior in his landmark decision of Marbury *v.* Madison. Thoreau and the Abolitionists converted protest into a massive bludgeon which, a century later, Gandhi would lift and wield with phenomenal success in the struggle for Indian independence. And—to return from the world scene to the microcosm of Joe's case—it was the clamorous force of a public protest that secured the pardon and opened the penitentiary gate for him.

In sum, protest is a democracy's most distinctive mode of evincing responsibility. While the other two (prevention and reparation) require courts, policemen, and soldiers, which are available even under despotic rule, protest requires only a democratic audience more or less sensitive, reasonable, and well-intentioned. That is why the very utterance of a protest constitutes an act of faith in the popular vindication of right and justice.

These then are prevention, reparation, and protest, the three great processes on the agenda of citizenship responsibility. And the greatest of them is—? For present purposes, it does not really matter very much. We need not choose; experience makes it obvious that we must continue to employ all three. Instead of awarding a laurel to one or another, we should do well to investigate the ways of making them more effectual in the daily operations of a responsible community.

### *Education in Collective Responsibility*

Sometimes it seems that our collective responsibilities, which result from the mere status of citizenship, are the most difficult to learn. According to the experience of the last two centuries, impulsions of responsibility do not come easily to democratic societies, and when they do come, they are unlikely to continue very long. Popular majorities appear to be excitable enough when confronted with an instance of injustice, but they tend to assume that all they owe the situation is a quick, hearty dab of remorse and reparation. Hence in a democracy most good things must be done well and thoroughly when first attempted or they may be neglected for an indefinite time. And since the average free citizen takes it for granted that all genuinely current issues, all truly modern thinkers, and all personally incumbent duties emerged after the date of his own thirteenth birthday and that anything earlier is good only for answers on history examinations, there is often a deficiency of continuity and learning to overcome the old imperial or official perspective.

While the official perspective is the chief and largest obstacle, it is certainly not the only one. Obviously, any proposal, any reform that imputes fallibility to elected officials is destined to meet with tough resistance on their part; seemingly, the only way to induce them to concede, even for purposes of argument, that they are capable of erring is to demonstrate, by one or many notorious instances in the past, that they have most indisputably erred. But officials are not the only ones. There are also many ordinary citizens who find difficulty in understanding the new political responsibility. As they see it, the notions of prevention, reparation, and protest may be desirable enough as ideals and in the abstract, but what if someone should take them literally and start applying them in such a way as to interfere with commerce or business?

For example, it will come as no great surprise that Joe and his friend and neighbor Ted (who was falsely identified and convicted along with him) lived in a slum area, i.e., an area where crimes of every kind, including the crimes committed by policemen, are more likely to breed. If a society is sincerely determined to prevent or at least reduce the incidence of tragedies like Joe's and Ted's, part of its agenda of responsibility will consist in a program of slum clearance and urban redevelopment. Of the many possible ways to attempt prevention, surely this is one of the soundest. But suppose, as so often occurs, the practical steps needed to effectuate it happen to interfere with an established business.

Max Morris owned and operated a department store in Washington, D.C. Though the neighborhood might not have been good for its residents, who were almost all Negroes, it was very good for Mr. Morris' business. Sixty-five per cent of the dwellings in the area were beyond repair, 58 per cent had outside toilets, 60 per cent had no baths, 29 per cent no electricity, 82 per cent no washbasins or laundry tubs, and 84 per cent no central heating. But all this did not seem to have any connection with Mr. Morris' property, which he used only for commercial purposes. Thus he went along from year to year as smoothly as possible—one does not expect complete serenity in a going business—buying and selling, hiring and firing, announcing his specials and his sales, saying what he thought about unions, the weather, and the government, displaying things here and hiding things there and generally attending to his own affairs.

He did and continued doing all these things and never quite realized how much he enjoyed them—until, one day, acting under authority of the District of Columbia Redevelopment Act, the National Capital Planning Commission and Redevelopment Agency decided to redevelop the entire "blighted" area and, for that purpose, to buy his property from him whether he wished to sell it or not. As soon as he could collect himself, Mr. Morris began a suit to have the whole Redevelopment Act declared unconstitutional, at least as far as it applied to him and his store.

In the trial court, his arguments met with considerable sympathy. While the decision held the Redevelopment Act to be constitutional, it put a narrow interpretation on the Agency's powers. The trial court thought that urban redevelopment was disagreeably newfangled:

> Let us suppose that the area is backward, stagnant, not properly laid out, economically Eighteenth Century—anything except detrimental to health, safety or morals. Suppose its owners and occupants like it that way. . . . In many circles all such views are considered "backward and stagnant." Are those who hold them "therefore blighted"? Can they not, nevertheless, own property? Choice of antiques is a right of property.

These phrases Mr. Morris must have read with approval and pleasure. Fortunately for his peace of mind, he did not live to see what would happen to the case when it reached the United States Supreme Court. There, not a single justice could be persuaded to suppose that people might prefer living in a blighted area because they "like it that way." Speaking for the unanimous Supreme Court, Justice William O. Douglas declared:

> Miserable and disreputable housing conditions may do more than spread disease and crime and immorality. They may also suffocate the spirit by reducing the people who live there to the status of cattle. They may indeed make living an almost insufferable burden. They may also

be an ugly sore, a blight on the community which robs it of charm, which makes it a place from which men turn. The misery of housing may despoil a community as an open sewer may ruin a river.

We do not sit to determine whether a particular housing project is or is not desirable. The concept of the public welfare is broad and inclusive. . . . The values it represents are spiritual as well as physical, aesthetic as well as monetary. It is within the power of the legislature to determine that the community should be beautiful as well as healthy, spacious as well as clean, well-balanced as well as carefully patrolled. . . .

The experts concluded that if the community were to be healthy, if it were not to revert again to a blighted or slum area, as though possessed of a congenital disease, the area must be planned as a whole. It was not enough, they believed, to remove existing buildings that were unsanitary or unsightly. It was important to redesign the whole area so as to eliminate the conditions that cause slums—the overcrowding of dwellings, the lack of parks, the lack of adequate streets and alleys, the absence of recreational areas, the lack of light and air, the presence of outmoded street patterns. It was believed that the piecemeal approach, the removal of individual structures that were offensive, would be only a palliative. The entire area needed redesigning so that a balanced, integrated plan could be developed for the region, including not only new homes but also schools, churches, parks, streets, and shopping centers. In this way it was hoped that the cycle of decay of the area could be controlled and the birth of future slums prevented. . . .

The rights of these property owners are satisfied when they receive that just compensation which the Fifth Amendment exacts as the price of the taking.

Collective acts of prevention would be easier to organize if the need were always as evident and immediate as it is when a fire breaks out, a burglar breaks in, or a murderer draws his weapon. But since social evils are rarely considerate enough to send advance notice that they will call at such and such an hour, effective prevention requires continual vigilance and sense of community. The lack of a developed sense of community is perhaps the most difficult impediment to overcome, for the very system in which a Mr. Morris makes his living will probably teach him to seek the special, if necessary at the cost of the general, welfare. Who has a right to reproach him for pursuing his own interest? As Abraham Lincoln said, "If you put the smallest gold coin over any verse of the Bible, you will not be able to read the verse." While we admire and commend the exceptional kind of merchant who tries to serve his community's noncommercial interests, we had better retain the lawful power to compel complete cooperation when we cannot secure it willingly. In short, Justice Douglas' eloquent sentences would have been scarcely necessary if there were not such a wide gap between the supreme law of American mercantile society and the supreme law of the land.

Nevertheless, Congress did pass the Redevelopment Act, the Agency did proceed to renew the blighted area, the Supreme Court did provide a constitutional support for the spiritual values of social existence, and the community did display its collective responsibility in planned measures of prevention. Of this and a wide variety of other preventive programs, Joe and his fellow victim Ted would undoubtedly approve. At least, redevelopment measures when properly and considerately administered are signs of hope and good faith. But when one leaves the processes of prevention and turns to what has been done to provide for reparation, there is much less cause for encouragement.

For one thing, since any adequate reparation in cases like Joe's and Ted's would necessarily include the community's disavowing the perpetrators of the outrage, it is dismaying to note how rarely any federal, state, or municipal official is discharged or punished for violating civil liberties. Even when a police commissioner finds it politic to rebuke a policeman publicly for using third-degree methods, he may, likely as not, cancel the rebuke with a private wink and a caution to leave no scars the next time. Seldom does a district attorney prosecute such a policeman. And—to culminate the blame—seldom does an American electorate vote a prosecutor out of office because he is known to violate the constitutional rights of accused persons.

Under a responsible system of law, a court trial is considered a success if it leads to a just outcome; in many American jurisdictions, it is considered a success only if it leads to a conviction. Frequently, the newspapers laud a prosecutor and the voters promote him according to the test that was used by the American aborigines—i.e., the number of scalps he has collected. Along with the others, Joe's scalp and Ted's count for two, at least until the truth about them chances to come to light, if it ever does. If we profess to give adequate reparation to victims like Joe and Ted, it is imperative that we inflict condign punishment on every offending official. There are quite a few prosecutors and policemen in the United States who belong on the other side of prison bars.

The national performance has not been creditable even in terms of money reparations. Ever since the eighteenth century, spokesmen of enlightened thought have been recommending that we adopt general laws which would grant money damages to persons unjustly imprisoned. First Voltaire, then Jeremy Bentham and Sir Samuel Romilly were among the early advocates. In the United States the honor of urging the reform goes to Edwin M. Borchard, Law Librarian of Congress and later professor of law at Yale University. Switzerland, the Scandinavian nations, and several other European countries adopted a variety of plans to compensate for erroneous convictions before the question was even seriously mooted in America. Borchard's plan, submitted to the United States Congress in 1912, was enacted by it into law (O admirable dispatch!) in 1938. A pathetically small list of states (for example, Wisconsin and California in 1913, North Carolina in 1947) heeded the zealous and scholarly appeals in which Borchard persevered as long as he lived.

Meanwhile, the old imperial perspective has persisted in most of our states, has afforded convenient protection for all vulnerable officials whose errors and crimes might be revealed if their victims were able to sue for compensation, and has furnished various petty politicians with a lucrative source of income. In the absence of a general compensatory statute, no one could publicize an outrage in court because no one could bring the state into court. The state, we are reminded, is "sovereign," hence immune from being sued without its consent. "You say the State has wronged you by an unjust imprisonment? Well, perhaps it has, although the notion is hard to conceive if one believes, as we officials do, that an act cannot really constitute a wrong unless we have recognized it as such and granted a remedy for it. Of course, you have no right to sue the sovereign. But if you petition us with sufficient humility, we may consider your case and pass a private appropriation bill to compensate you. This is not a promise. It is only a possibility, which you can readily destroy for yourself either by failing to retain John Wardheeler Doe as your advocate or by complaining too emotionally about your treatment, some years since, by our political ally, District Attorney Richard Grafter Roe. Be discreet, my friend, and the legislature may eventually grant you grace."

Such is the posture of affairs in most of our states. The private bills come in from term to term. Mood, caprice, influence, political chicane—almost any factor can determine the result except rational recognition of desert. Many of the humble applicants are turned away empty-handed, with no reason assigned. For an example of caprice, there is Joe's own case, which arose in the State of Illinois. Joe, who was held in prison for twelve years, was voted a special appropriation of $24,000. Ted, falsely convicted in the very same trial, was kept in prison for another five years, released on a court's writ of habeas corpus, and voted no reparation whatever.

Nevertheless, there remains the meager comfort of the general federal and state laws that Borchard inspired. Cannot one feel that these, at least, represent the full and ethical performance of a collective responsibility? It would be pleasant to say "yes," for the several laws do acknowledge our collective duties, they are substantially sound in principle. But the candid answer must be "no," for each of them contains a flaw which greatly impairs its usefulness. When Borchard submitted his plan to the congressmen in 1912, he was understandably eager to assure them that, if adopted, it would not cost the government very much. With this end in view, he provided in the draft bill that no victim of injustice should be awarded more than a certain specified number of dollars by way of reparation. Quite a while before, Aristotle had warned explicitly against the dangers of clauses like this one. He had pointed out that the value of a currency unit might gradually shrink so much that a specified sum (maximum or minimum) suitable at one epoch might become entirely unsuitable at another. Nevertheless, anxious for the reform, Borchard proceeded to specify a maximum of $5,000, i.e., not the equivalent in current purchasing power of 5,000 1912 dollars, but the sum of $5,000 pure and simple. He made no allowance for the possibility of future inflation. Congress and the state legislatures adopted his draft, and what was once a respectable maximum has gradually shrunk in value until it jeopardizes the utility of the entire scheme.

Under the circumstances, it is indispensable that congressmen and the state legislators pay heed to the other half of Aristotle's remarks on the subject. He advised that if a lawmaker did rely on specifying sums of money to establish a legislative classification, he must periodically review the amounts and adjust them to the currency's changing value. This is one solution; there are several others which might be considered if the legislatures would give the matter attention. As matters stand, what an embarrassing tableau the nation has to contemplate! On one side, one sees the majority of the states behaving fitfully, capriciously, and unequally —degrading the name of grace; on the other, one sees the federal government and a few states conducting themselves quite justly in point of principle and quite unjustly in point of dollars; downstage, one still seems to descry Edwin M. Borchard, pleading from the grave on behalf of fairness and civic honor.

There is little in the scene to feed an American's sense of patriotic satisfaction. Nevertheless, despite the embarrassment, we must not become confused about the nature of the collective involvement. We must not confound community neglect and default with *primary* guilt. While the electorate can be said to have failed and defaulted, failed to respond to the Voltaire-Bentham-Borchard appeal, defaulted in its duty to compensate for the unjust imprisonments, these are the limits of the moral reproach it must bear. It did not perpetrate the initial injustice, nor did it encourage or approve it. The prosecutor and policemen are the ones who caused the tragedy and incurred the burden of guilt; there is no reason for the community to diminish their guilt by sharing it. The default on the community's part does not have retroactive moral consequences; it does not implicate the outsiders—the mass of mere electors—in an offense which took place years before they had occasion to suspect the doing of official wrong.

How do we appear as a people when one passes from the processes of reparation to those of public protest? Protest, as we have seen, is democracy's own distinctive mode of demonstrating civic responsibility. Out of prudence, a despotic regime may take measures to *prevent* injustices, or at least the injustices that appear useless to it; out of policy, it may offer *reparation* for injustices that are disclosed provided the mode of disclosing does not embarrass someone currently in favor; but it will not dare to maintain open channels for free public *protest.* Free protest and despotism can never live together anywhere; one must inevitably drive the other out. And what shall we say is the American record?

Generally speaking, the law in America has been rather more receptive than the social community to free expression and protest. Again and again in our annals, a local community has reacted intolerantly, repressively, even murderously toward those who avowed dissenting and unpopular opinions. The incidents are not confined to conflicts between one race and another, nor are they confined to the Southern states where violence always seems latent and ready to explode. In addition, there are social ostracisms to cope with, professional black-listings, and economic boycotts, that is, alternative ways by which the dominant majority may subdue a stubborn dissenter. It is not unknown that a dissenter's children, ridiculed and persecuted by their schoolmates, have grown hostile to him and intensified the total pressure. Most of our small communities are by no means adequately attached to the principles of the Bill of Rights. On the other hand, the national community generally—not always—conducts itself in a more civilized manner.

Take the case of J. M. Near, a man who appears to have made

a checkered career for himself out of publishing defamatory and scurrilous weekly newspapers. The *Saturday Press,* which he published for a while in Minneapolis, featured articles attacking the Jews. Somehow one gathers the impression that Near was one of those who pander to anti-Semitism mainly because it is a profitable way to make a living and because, as they explain, others would do it if they did not. There are individuals everywhere who seem born for this kind of work. While still in the carefree years of high school, they begin by purveying advance copies of examination answers, obscene pictures, and marijuana cigarettes; then they graduate to more ambitious varieties of merchandise. To please the kind of following it had, the *Saturday Press* would probably have engaged in attacks on Catholics, Negroes, Japanese, or Masons with the same ratio of logic to zeal that it exhibited against the Jews.

In a series of weekly issues, Near, who admitted to a reputation tainted with suspicion of blackmail, chose to vilify and bespatter the mayor of Minneapolis, the county attorney, the chief of police, the representative of the citizens' law-enforcement league, certain members of the current grand jury, and, of course, the "Jewish Race." If one could credit the *Saturday Press,* all of these, including the "Jewish Race," were conspiring to protect a Jewish gangster who was supposed to control the local gambling and racketeering. Though using the cloacal style that is typical of such papers, the *Saturday Press* did not incite its readers to riot against the alleged conspirators but merely to abhor and revile them.

At length, the county attorney (Floyd B. Olson, who was later to become the esteemed governor of the state) brought a civil suit against J. M. Near and the *Saturday Press* to have the newspaper abated as a public nuisance. A Minnesota statute authorized the courts to forbid and enjoin the business of publishing "a malicious, scandalous and defamatory newspaper." The statute also provided that a publisher could defeat such an action by showing "that the truth was published with good motives and for justifiable ends."

At the trial of the case, Near offered no evidence at all. The trial court decided that he had made a business of publishing a malicious, scandalous, and defamatory newspaper, and it forbade and enjoined him from continuing the nuisance. After a unanimous affirmance in the Minnesota Supreme Court, Near appealed to the Supreme Court of the United States.

It can fairly be said that if ever the circumstances might tempt a court to employ the old official perspective, this was the case. Near's way of exercising the freedom of the press had virtually no social value. If anything, it was harmful. On the other hand, a decision suppressing his defamation would not only serve to reduce religious and other tensions; it would also protect honorable officials against false scandals and thus help the community to recruit better candidates for municipal service. It was a hard case for the constitutional right of protest.

Yet the United States Supreme Court decided (5 to 4) that the Minnesota statute and the injunction against Near were unconstitutional. Possibly Near might be subject to suit for civil damages; in appropriate circumstances he might even be prosecuted for criminal libel *after* publishing defamatory material; but in no event could he be enjoined *before* publication. No American publisher could be put in the position of having to satisfy any official, including a judge, that his motives in publishing were good and justifiable, at the peril of having his newspaper abated as a public nuisance. The Minnesota statute attempted to impose a *previous* restraint on publishers, and this, said Chief Justice Hughes for the Court, "This is of the essence of censorship."

Yet were not Near's accusations scandalous? Yes, they assuredly were, said the Chief Justice. "Charges of reprehensible conduct, and in particular of official malfeasance, unquestionably create a public scandal, but the theory of the constitutional guaranty is that even a more serious public evil would be caused by authority to prevent publication." Yet were not these accusations of Near's also totally false? Granted that they were, there would still be no ground for a decree of previous restraint. The community had the fundamental right to hear the accusations as they were published and to determine the extent of their truth or falsity for itself. It could not legislate to strip itself of that right. Whether or not Near's freedom of expression protected him from damage suits and criminal prosecutions after the fact, a restraint before publication would deprive not only Near but the community as well.

Thus the court majority adhered to the classic libertarian assumptions about the common people's good sense, practical acumen, and capacity to recognize a fraud when they see one. As we have already noticed, there is scarcely enough favorable evidence in our history to make one feel sanguine about the assumptions. The people have used very bad judgment on various important occasions, and sometimes they have succumbed to such rabid hysteria that they cannot be said to have used any judgment at all. Consequently, certain sophisticated observers in our day are wont to call the Bill of Rights an unrealistic and doctrinaire eighteenth century instrument—idealistic perhaps but no longer workable. What shall we reply?

There are several replies available. For one thing, if the people err, so too do all officials at one time or another, and the only way of making them acknowledge their fallibility is to use—and if need be, abuse—the right of protest. Surely what will, at the final outcome, prove a true use and what will prove a false abuse can scarcely be known before the unfolding of the event. For one thing, the people do respond—though not so reasonably as Jefferson and Madison hoped—to the assumption that they can judge and discriminate for themselves. The assumption about the people's judgment operates as a type of self-fulfilling prediction. If we say as we do, "Give a dog a bad name and he'll bite," it seems only fair to add, "Give him a good name and he'll guard your possessions," and presumably it is the latter, more optimistic attitude that justifies our freedom of popular discussion and protest.

Yet, solid as these reasons are, we need not be satisfied to rest with them. There is something more to the justification of free protest, something that men are prone to overlook because it is below the surface like a foundation which penetrates deep in the ground and supports the entire visible fabric. It is the simple, massive fact that the people are the consumers of law and government. If they cannot eventually judge between political true and political false (not necessarily at first glance or even at second, but eventually), then the blunders they commit are the very ones they must consume. If they persistently prefer tinsel to gold, tinsel is what they must live with. If their government invites them to choose freely at the risk of making their own mistakes, they may gradually learn from the mistakes to choose more wisely. But—let us insist on it—even if they do not learn, even if they should repeat the same old stupidities again and again, no one could rightly dispute their title to make the ultimate political choices. No one, not even they themselves, not all of them now living. For this right—the right to protest, hear, deliberate, and choose—is not only an organ of the Given which our past has bequeathed, not only an organ of the Created which our present is shaping, it is also an organ of the Promise which we necessarily transmit to the future. At any single moment, the men of a community may freely refuse to listen to any voice, but they have no power to decide that they or their descendants will never thereafter wish to hear it.

On the legal front, there have been advances and retreats since 1931 when Near's case was decided. In the interval, some Americans have grown chary of our traditional free assumptions, while others have learned to prize them with greater devotion. Almost all would agree, however, that without a great deal of uninhibited communication, there can be no genuine community in democratic life. The consumer perspective simply could not be maintained under a system of repression and censorship.

And now it is appropriate to ask about a certain deep motif that seems to have emerged whenever we referred to the moral existence of a social community. In whatever aspect we considered the subject of electoral responsibility, we ran into a recurrence of the same idea, which beats and repeats through our analysis like a *basso ostinato*. It is the theme of mutual sharing or allotting or distributing. Whether our topic dealt with prevention (*e.g.*, Mr. Morris' involuntary experience in sharing), with reparation (*e.g.*, the legislatures' failure to provide for sharing through compensatory laws), or with protest (*e.g.*, the necessity of sharing political views and information), we have continued to meet the same emphatic theme. What is the pertinence of sharing? As electors in a modern democratic community, when do we morally oblige ourselves to share?

### *Responsibility in Community Enterprise*

Our analysis has been leading us toward a fundamental democratic principle which we may call "the general principle of community enterprise." It is: Whenever a community establishes an organ or embarks on an enterprise in order to fulfill one of its purposes, it is obliged, as far as it is able, to compensate any member who is unwarrantably injured in the course of the operation. The obligation should be reckoned as an incidental expense in providing a social service. Whether it is assumed in the price of the service or in the general budget of the government, the cost of reparation should be spread as extensively as practicable through the community. In cases of unjust imprisonment, like Joe's and Ted's, the community ought to pay not only because it can more readily bear the economic burden; it ought to pay because one of its own enterprises inflicted the injury.

In stating this principle, we should take care to notice that it does not rest merely on the moral fault of government officials, nor is it restricted to injuries caused by them deliberately or corruptly. Joe and Ted deserved reparation because they had suffered as immediate consumers of a community enterprise. It made little or no practical difference to them whether the prosecution's chief witness identified them dishonestly or honestly, corruptly or mistakenly as long as her identification induced the jury to convict them. An honest error on her part, far from shortening their years in the penitentiary, would have been equally unjust to them and, in all probability, more difficult to uncover and correct. In a consumer's perspective, the injustice is complete whenever an innocent man is punished. Sincere but mistaken identifications occur much more frequently than dishonest ones, and appear to inflict much more harm.

The federal and state reparation laws, based on Borchard's draft, are sensible enough to provide compensation on proof of an unjust imprisonment, and no one is required to demonstrate that a particular official planned the injustice. As regards a claim for compensation, the injustice can remain entirely and permanently "anonymous." How it befell and who caused it to befall are questions for the community and the government to investigate; it is for them to fix the blame, to punish the guilty officials, and to install preventive arrangements; but the proving of official guilt has no material bearing on the victim's right to reparation. Following similar reasoning, a New York State law provides that if a city policeman should summon a bystander to help him catch a criminal and the bystander should be injured or killed while assisting, the city must compensate for the damages—without anyone's having to prove negligence or fault on the part of the police.

As we see, the principle of community enterprise has been making inroads on the obsolete belief that states are immune from being charged with wrong or being obliged to make reparation. Ever since the latter half of the nineteenth century, the pose of hiding behind "sovereign immunity" has become less and less convincing. The old screen, once so comfortably opaque, is now translucent in some spots, transparent in others; as an excuse for denying reparation, it does not even serve the uses of hypocrisy.

For generations, a number of progressive jurists (Professor Borchard among them) repeatedly urged the United States Congress and the state legislatures to enact not only provisions for the unjustly convicted but also general "tort claims acts," i.e., laws by which the "sovereign" would consent to be sued for civil injuries which might be inflicted in the course of its operations and enterprises. At length, in 1929 New York led the way with a state tort claims act. Not until 1946 did the national Congress follow. It is a woeful fact that more than half of our states still have no such legislation. The British Parliament responded to the movement as late as 1947.

Unfortunately, in framing and adopting this obvious reform, there was more than the fallacy of sovereign immunity to overcome. There was also the problem of deciding what legal obligations ought to be borne by the state in cases of private injuries. Should the courts treat the state as they would treat a man and judge its conduct as they would judge a man's?

On this point, the French, who were considerably ahead of the English and Americans in time, were even farther ahead in justice. French courts recognized the fatuous old anthropomorphic fallacy, and they would have none of it. Almost a century ago, they decided that the state's liability for injuries should not be measured by the same rules which define an individual's liability. Having been established by the community to perform certain assigned functions, the state should be judged according to the way it performs them. It should be liable for the injuries it might cause through functioning poorly. Defective state service is no less harmful when we do not know and cannot prove precisely what went wrong, i.e., when the malfunctioning remains "anonymous."

In America and in England, these astute observations were sadly overlooked. The typical American statute provides that the government shall be liable for injuries "in the same manner and to the same extent as a private individual under like circumstances." With this sort of legislation, the government's colossal capacity to inflict injury grossly exceeds its legal responsibility. One might say the congressmen had seen too many political cartoons and had legislated for the United States of America as for an old man with a farmer's beard, a twinkle in his eye, a stovepipe hat, and an old-fashioned suit made of stars and stripes.

Under the American legislation, the state assumes the duties not of a government but of a private individual. If a rookie policeman at the scene of a holdup should shoot the victim of the holdup instead of the robber, the victim would not recover compensation from the city unless he could prove it was negligent in some specific respect, say, in training the policeman—though, curiously enough, his wound feels just the same either way. Without proof of an anthropomorphic "fault," an adventitious loss caused by an American community enterprise will not be distributed throughout the community but will remain, as it falls, on one member only.

This condition of the law plays a particularly embarrassing role in connection with novel enterprises and experiments. One would ordinarily expect that officials were required to exert particular care in installing a new, experimental project and that when an injury resulted from it, the courts would be quick to hold the state liable. According to common sense, the more novel the enterprise, the more evident the need of special care. But the governing rule of law is precisely the reverse. According to most of our judges, including some who are usually leaders of liberal jurisprudence, the courts should avoid finding the state at fault in these circumstances because state liability might frighten the officials into abandoning humane experiments and returning to the cruder methods of the past.

The reasoning of the judges is very old and characteristically predemocratic. Pharaoh might argue that he could not build a pyramid unless the populace subsidized the undertaking with their labors and their lives, Louis XIV might argue the same way about the building of Versailles, and the magnates of the nineteenth century about the building of industrial factories and transcontinental railroads. To us the excuse rings thin. Subsidies in adventitious private suffering are unwelcome to a modern democratic community, which wishes to go on with its social ascent but is averse to clambering over corpses. If it is true that every progressive experiment involves a certain risk of incidental injuries, surely a democratic community will be just, generous, and proud enough to insist on reimbursing those who have paid the toll.

Let me give a concrete instance. A man by the name of William Kennedy had been convicted of attempted robbery, had been sent to New York State's Elmira Reformatory, had been paroled, had been sent back to prison for violating his parole, and was then transferred to Auburn Prison. The Auburn prison farm, situated about four miles east of the prison, is administered under regulations known as "minimum security."

On the first day that Kennedy was assigned to the farm, and within hours after his arrival there, he disappeared. He was one of thirty-two prisoners on the farm, working under the supervision of one of the two guards on duty. Both guards were unarmed. The farm had no fence around it, nor was it provided with pickets, towers, or lookouts. The prisoners were at times permitted to do their work out of sight of the guards, and as soon as Kennedy found himself in this position, he fled. Though the prison farm, located on a road leading to a state highway, was provided with a siren, the siren was not sounded, nor was any road block set up.

Somehow—we cannot know just how—Kennedy got into the truck of one Albert Williams, a local farmer, and by use of threats compelled Williams to help him escape. Half an hour later, Williams, with Kennedy at his side, halted the truck for a few seconds at a gas station, tried by gestures to signal for help, then drove on. A few minutes later, a neighbor saw the truck go by and wondered why Albert Williams was driving so fast. He observed there was a strange man beside him in the front seat. Another forty-five minutes passed. The truck stopped, and Kennedy, the escaped convict, took flight. Williams was found sitting on the running board, acutely ill. Taken to a hospital, he died the next day by reason of a brain hemorrhage caused by the terror to which he had been subjected.

The convict was soon apprehended. When he was caught, he was carrying a sweater which Williams had been wearing and a sharp blade, six inches long, taken from the prison farm. This is the extent of our knowledge of the last day of Albert Williams' life.

The New York tribunal exonerated the state for the wrongful death of Albert Williams. Two grounds were assigned for denying liability: (1) Although the state employees were concededly negligent in allowing Kennedy to escape, there was nothing in his previous record to indicate "that he was likely to wander from the prison and assault members of the public"; and (2) If responsibility were imposed on the state in a case like this, wardens and prison keepers would be deterred from continuing their experiments with "minimum security." The widow's judgment in the amount of $16,800 was set aside and her claim was dismissed.

Here we are dealing with a problem of national magnitude. For example, escapes from a model prison in California conducted on the method of "minimum security" run to about 5 per cent per annum. The peril is not small. In the vicinity of various penal and psychiatric institutions, the cases show that strange and violent things may happen to housewives who answer their doorbells after dark. Of course, this does not mean that every fugitive will resort to physical violence, for many of them do no harm whatever. It means that, since the penological and psychiatric experts agree that flight can transform a man's personality, no one can possibly predict how a mental defective or a convict—even one who is usually docile—will behave if he escapes, becomes a fugitive, and thinks of himself as a quarry of huntsmen.

It is entirely proper for a community to feel solicitous on behalf of penological advances, custodial reforms, and experimental methods in public institutions. If its solicitude is sincere, it can scarcely cavil over paying a claim of $16,800 for a human life destroyed incidentally in the course of an experimental enterprise. In the war against social maladies, we may or may not prevail, but we can certainly share the cost of trying.

It is time for all democratic governments to cease restricting their responsibility, like a human individual's, to specific instances of negligence, wrongdoing, or "fault." It is time to acknowledge that the question of the state's anthropomorphic negligence was not really interesting to Mr. Williams during those last hours of his; for him, it sufficed that the convict Kennedy had escaped. What confronted him was not a problem of efficient prison administration, but a personal disaster as inexorable as it was anonymous. And in this regard Williams' tragic death epitomized a large and momentous portion of all our destinies. In the end, after the label of fault has been applied in so many places and failed so often to adhere, after it has fallen away and gradually lost its color and its lettering, some among us come to acknowledge that the solacing of ill may be far more important than the placing of blame. How much of blame is ultimately fruitless to impute and how much of ill remains at last anonymous—the pain of one, the fault of none, and the decent concern of all!

In our survey of democratic involvement, we have begun by examining the limited or minimum responsibilities which are incumbent on mere electors. On the one hand, it has been comforting to find that mere electors are not automatically implicated in the guilts of official misconduct. On the other hand, it has been discomforting to find so many gaps between what genuine collective responsibility demands and what American law actually provides to foster the processes of prevention, reparation, and protest.

In the light of what we have called "the general principle of community enterprise," our shortcomings and defaults seem discreditable. We find the respective statutes of reparation maladroit in certain American jurisdictions, fallacious in others, and totally absent in many. To this extent, democratic citizens are failing their minimum collective responsibilities.

The default will not be cured by depending on lawyers for action. There are good and bad, wise and foolish, honest and dishonest lawyers—every conceivable kind, in fact, except the kind who can relieve their fellow citizens of attending personally to elementary civic obligations. More accurately and honestly than anything we may profess, our statutes and laws articulate the moral values in practical operation within our society. Thus it is not a legal code but a civilization we are assessing.

# IV

## Citizenship: Individual Responsibilities

### The Guilt of Accessories

If democracy is sufficiently extensive and influential to be considered a world-wide type of civilization, is it justifiable on our part to concentrate so much of our analysis on the United States of America, a fragment of the democratic cosmos? Why do we not turn our light more often on other democratic countries? In essence, our purpose in concentrating on the United States has been sociological. That is to say, the United States is not only the most powerful of the democratic nations, it is also the one where religious, ethnic, and racial differences are presented most dramatically and where the tensions induced by democracy's encounter with the spread of communism have been most clearly defined. If we respect reason and science, we cannot mingle the data of one society indiscriminately with the data of another, nor can we disregard the fact that a precept of law derives most of its practical meaning from its own social and institutional context. As for readers in other countries, they will not fail to recognize how often our analysis relates directly to them.

But why so much preoccupation with laws and court decisions? Here we are, repeatedly turning to positive laws and concrete instances instead of following the traditional path to the upper philosophical regions where theorists can rest at ease, disregard the distant swarms in the humid valley, and send forth utterances of absolute and universal validity. Most of the literature of moral and political philosophy has been composed on just such heights, which may explain why it comprises so many unqualified pronouncements. Thinkers who talk from the heights are safer when they remain there.

Perhaps the most we can claim for our chosen road—which runs along the floor of valley after valley—is that we usually bring our merchandise back to the same market of concrete human experience where we found the raw materials. If, in the course of our progress, we succeed in processing some specific combination of laws, decisions and civic behavior into a generalized statement (which will almost never aspire to perfect or universal validity), the empirical criteria of our meaning are at hand for anyone to observe and use.

While laws and legal decisions cannot tell the whole story of government and its influence on a people's life, they do clearly reveal the directions in which the society is moving, the standards it professes, the relative degrees of public sincerity and hypocrisy, and the price the people are willing to pay to preserve the values they proclaim. The writings of the ancient Hebrews and Greeks are replete with the proposition that the law is a lamp unto the feet and a light unto the path so that good laws make for a good society and bad laws are a curse and reproach to the people. Even the Romans, who were infinitely better at managing things than at comprehending them, were able to see that a regime should be appreciated in terms of its laws, and when Augustus died, the Senate ordered that his funeral procession, which was conducted through a gate of triumph, be headed by the titles of the laws enacted during his reign. In other words, laws deserve our special notice because they enunciate the society.

As far as American society is concerned, we have been preoccupied in Chapter III with the "outer chamber" of citizenship, by which we mean the area of responsibility that includes all adult citizens without regard to distinctions and differences among them. The outer chamber is the place of collective responsibilities. Through it one must pass before he is equipped to consider his position in the "inner chamber," which is the place of individual and distinctive responsibilities. In the outer chamber, a man is considered a "mere" citizen, an integer, a member of the electorate like anyone else. As he enters the inner chamber, his civic responsibilities and guilts become individualized. The guilts of the inner chamber arise—if they arise at all—not from a status of mere citizenship but from the distinctive facts of his own personal biography.

What with the profuse variety that obtains among personalities, consciences, and destinies, it seems we shall be hard put to install any sort of rational order in studying the inner chamber. How can one hope to define criteria which will evaluate so many different and such intensely private experiences? In Chapter III we dealt with the general fact patterns which determine collective responsibility, and they were relatively few; but here, by definition, we have come to a place where most of the decisive facts are not only disparate from person to person but also, in most instances, strictly private.

I think it is this element of privacy in the dilemma that indicates the way we should proceed for the time being. Whenever in any inquiry some decisive circumstance happens to be held privately, those engaged in the inquiry can adopt one of two courses. The easy course is to disregard the inconvenient circumstance, adopt a wholly behavioristic method, and thereby invite a plunge into error. The alternative and more difficult course consists in inviting the person who has been the object of the inquiry to become one of its subjects by cooperating in a process of self-search. After all, every philosophy is based on the postulate that because a man chooses to fish from the pier, there must be some fish in the lake, and this postulate is bold enough without our assuming further that someone else will catch, cook, and season the fish and that we need merely sit at the table and eat it. There is no ready-made external formula for the problems of individual civic responsibility. The sole available recourse is a sincere internal search predicated on the series of questions we are about to list. Of necessity the questions will be offensive to some and irksome to almost all. Fortunate is the citizen who, after considering them rigorously in the forum of his conscience, can exonerate himself on every count.

## The Citizen's Self-Search: To Test Accessory Guilt

### *First. Did I incite the official to commit a wrong?*

In answering these questions, it is important to confine oneself to clear, proximate, and direct involvements, and to dismiss those that are intricate, abstruse, or remote. If one's personal connection with a given case seems to require a line of subtle or metaphysical reasoning to support it, one may rightly give himself the benefit of reasonable doubts. The search we have been proposing is not intended to encourage citizens in a morbid preoccupation with borderline or imaginary states of guilt. On the other hand, when a clear and manifest instance does arise, there is nothing but sophistry in pleading that if the circumstances had only been a little closer to the borderline, the answer might have been doubtful. Doubt about dusk is not doubt about noon.

For example, officials are incited to do *immediate* wrong whenever the press prejudges the outcome of a criminal prosecution, dehumanizes the person accused, clamors for his conviction and punishment, sensationalizes the trial, and lashes the community into hysterical passion. There is incitement to do wrong whenever the newspapers or the voters honor a prosecuting official not for his integrity in obtaining verdicts of justice but for his ruthlessness in obtaining verdicts of guilt. As we saw in the case of Joe and Ted, this kind of incitement may emanate from associations of local merchants, bankers, and property owners. Or the undue pressure may come from the leaders of self-styled "patriotic" associations. Whatever the source, those who incite officials to commit an act of wrong incur the guilt of moral accessories

### *Second. Did I authorize the wrong?*

This question relates to one's involvement with laws and legal institutions that are unjust in themselves. As we saw in Chapter III, the general community cannot be considered as participating in an official wrong if the official wrong itself violates established laws. Under such circumstances, we may be obliged to provide collective restitution but we are not burdened with the guilt of accessories. For example, the electors and representatives of the community had no reason to blush for the laws (against burglary and homicide) under which Joe and Ted were prosecuted. By voting for these laws, they certainly did not authorize anyone to use them against unoffending persons.

But suppose the vote is not so innocent. Suppose, in a state or local election, one of the candidates openly recommends a program of racial or religious discrimination while his opponent proposes to uphold the moral and constitutional standard of human equality. Under the circumstances, a vote for the former candidate does constitute an authorization and does involve the voter in accessory guilt. Of course, if a voter should commit an act of racial or religious oppression in the course of his own personal behavior, he would be no mere accessory but a principal in wrongdoing.

These, one can see, are the principles to be applied by a German voter in determining his own moral relation to the crimes of the Hitler regime. Let us assume he recognizes the collective obligation of the German nation to make whatever restitution or reparation it can, and let us assume further that he did not become a principal in wickedness by personally executing any of Hitler's crimes. Ought, then, this ordinary German citizen hold himself guilty of having been accessory to Hitler simply because he possessed a right to vote? Did he authorize Hitler's radical evil, the exterminations, the genocides, the gas chambers?

In moral terms, it makes no substantial difference whether our ordinary German actually knew about the gas chambers during the years of World War II when they were doing their work. He probably did not know, and even if he had known at that late stage, he would have been quite powerless to interfere. Few citizens did know, still fewer chose to know; yet, after the Nazi regime had fallen and the reign of hell had come to an end, many a conscientious German could not convince himself that his wartime ignorance exculpated him in the forum of conscience. The anxiety of the better German continues even now. Whatever others may have protested in order to evade their complicity, he feels the need to go on searching for self-exoneration or self-condemnation. If his moral position still seems ambiguous, there is a decisive way for him to resolve it. His immediate question is whether he had *previously* authorized the gas chambers.

The answer to this question will vary from mind to mind, conscience to conscience, and biography to biography. One man may exonerate himself because he once took occasion to exhibit sympathy and regret to a Jew or a Pole somewhere along the route to annihilation; another may recall an identical gesture and interpret it as demonstrating his guilty awareness of what was being done in the name of the nation. In the end, every German who was an adult during the Hitler period sits in judgment on himself and lives with his own answer; none requires us to serve as a court of moral appeal.

On the facts known to the outside world, there is only one category of Germans who could not possibly claim a rational basis for exonerating themselves as accessories. Those in this category stand guilty beyond reasonable doubt. They are the ones who, after reading *Mein Kampf* or becoming acquainted with its content and tenor in some other way, used their votes, money, or influence to assist Hitler's rise to the chancellorship. *Mein Kampf* was too explicit in its cult of extermination; it told the Germans far too precisely what a Nazi Germany would attempt. Even the gas chambers were explicated for all to read. More than once the book attacked the Kaiser's regime for not having thrust thousands of Jews into gas chambers at at the outbreak of World War I in 1914. Thus, when Hitler built the gas chambers for use in World War II, he was using authority that he had candidly sought and that his pre-1933 supporters had collaborated in conferring. Of course, the accessory guilt of such persons is neither contagious nor hereditary.

### *Third. Was I reckless in helping to install a conspicuously dangerous public instrument?*

Though, here again, we may be tempted to point to the Germans of 1932–33 and their reckless installation of the Nazi regime, it will be better for us to avoid complacency and concentrate on American affairs. We are notoriously careless in the way we choose magistrates and prosecutors, often preferring colorful personality to competence, brashness to common honesty, and the "right" ethnic origin to intelligence. Once in a while, an American community will reelect a mayor or legislator while he is serving a prison term for some venal offense. We choose state judges with almost no public investigation of their qualities. For example, the great judge Benjamin N. Cardozo (of Sephardic Jewish descent) owed his election to newly naturalized Italian-Americans who, seeing his name for the first time on the ballot, imagined it was Italian and gave him their votes.

In testing ourselves on this score, we need not follow a counsel of perfection. We need not convict ourselves of complicity in wrongdoing unless the guilty official was "conspicuously dangerous" at the time of his election. While bar associations are reasonably expected to have more information and exercise greater civic prudence in this regard, the remainder of us should at least notice dangers that stare us in the face. If we do not, there will be more district attorneys like the one who prosecuted Joe and Ted.

### *Fourth. Did I remain silent or passive when I might have prevented a wrong about to be perpetrated?*

There are many current instances of this kind of accessory guilt. For one of the clearest, take the position of a resident of some small town in Mississippi who learns that a mob is forming to lynch a Negro prisoner and that the sheriff and jailer are deliberately leaving the prison unguarded. The considerations which go to determine one's course in a position like this may help to illuminate other, less dramatic problems. Three factors are patent: (1) it is always more efficacious to prevent a wrong than to repair it; (2) a citizen should take greater risks if the threatened wrong happens by its very nature to be irreparable; and (3) we have a moral right to require courage of others but heroism only of ourselves.

### *Fifth. Did I ratify the act of wrong or knowingly accept its fruits?*

For example, American Communists shamelessly ratified innumerable atrocities committed under the regime of Josef Stalin.

For another example, during the Mussolini regime certain professors in Italian universities willingly accepted promotion to positions made vacant by the universities' discharging other professors who subscribed to anti-fascist doctrines. Thus a subsequent approval or ratification need not be spelled out explicitly. If a German criticizes Hitler today only because of the invasion of Russia or the loss of World II, he may be understood to ratify the Nazi crimes.

### *Sixth. Did I suppress the truth when it came to my notice and thus become an accessory after the fact?*

Oddly enough, suppressing the truth about a past wrong can work greater harm than excusing or defending it. While apologies may incidentally expose the underlying facts, which an audience, a class, or a public may evaluate as it sees fit, a policy of silence or suppression will inter everything together, put the wrong out of sight, stifle the victim, and annul the sense of injustice. In Germany, the most insidious way for a Nazi-minded professor to defend Hitler under present conditions is to tell young students nothing about him and let them assume—as most young students will—that atrocities they have not heard of must be either inconsequential or fictitious. In any country, the shrewdest way to prove that faceless informers are indispensable to the safety of the state is to refuse all information concerning them and hope that voters will infer—as some of them will—that the refusal of information is somehow more informative than information itself.

The refusal impresses many and frustrates the rest. It keeps people from learning facts that might serve "to disturb public confidence." It safeguards orderliness even if at a certain cost in justice. Voters who do not discover embarrassing facts cannot proceed to employ them for disrespectful purposes. As the Emperor Tiberius observed, whose expertness on the subject is not to be challenged, "Better subvert the Constitution than remove its guardians" (*Subverterent potius iura quam custodes eorum amoverent*). Here is the real meaning of the old official perspective, in stark epitome.

One further comment. He who suppresses an act of official wrong becomes something more than an accessory after the fact. In addition, he becomes an accessory before the fact of subsequent, similar wrongs. His silence, which buries the completed act of injustice, smooths the path to other offenses in the future. Because of him, official wrong comes to seem insignificant, then safe, and at last quite right. His is an unenviable role.

### *Seventh. Before the wrong was committed, had I contributed to the vulnerability of the victim?*

In the kingdom of the strong it is a crime to be weak. People like Joe and Ted are likely to become involved with the police because they live in poor neighborhoods, have no influential friends, cannot pay skillful lawyers, shift from job to job or from job to unemployment—in short, because they are vulnerable. Their condition continually tempts the unscrupulous among policemen and prosecutors. If they are unlucky, they find themselves accused because they are vulnerable and convicted because they are accused. When they fall into trouble, they are less likely to be believed; their case enlists no interest or curiosity; their predicament seems entirely normal to the reporters, the judge, the jury, and the appellate court. What to them is calamity is to everyone else mere mechanical routine, and all because they began by being vulnerable.

Who makes such people vulnerable? In some instances, it may be the vicious neighbors, in others the family, and in still others no one but the victims themselves and their personal weaknesses. Again, it may be the slum landlords and the corrupt politicians who exploit the needs of the poor. Each case of official wrong has its own distinct economic background and its own roster of persons who became accessories by contributing to the victim's vulnerability.

As we live in an age of the mingling of races and churning of cultures, it is appropriate to underscore one specific class of accessory guilt, that is, the guilt of racial, religious, and ethnic discriminations. The owners of real property, the employers, the union leaders who discriminate on these grounds are all proximate contributors to the vulnerability of those whom they exclude.

### *The Self-Search in Operation*

In order to illustrate its usefulness, let me give one or two direct examples of the citizen's Self-Search at work. Each of the incidents I am about to recount involved inhumane behavior on the part of the Immigration Service under the control and supervision of the Attorney General of the United States. At the time, the responsible department heads were Attorney General (now Justice) Tom Clark and his successor, Attorney General J. Howard McGrath.

At the end of World War II, Congress adopted the War Brides Act which, by way of reward to men who had served honorably in the armed forces, permitted them to bring their alien wives and children to the United States without regard to immigration quotas. Relying on the law, Kurt Knauff, an American soldier, sent his wife, Ellen, to New York. Of German birth and Czechoslovakian nationality, she had fled the Nazi regime in its early years. During and after the war she had served commendably in the British Royal Air Force and as civilian employee of the American Occupation

Forces. The American military and civilian authorities had screened and approved her application before she left Europe. When she arrived at New York in August, 1948, she was denied entry into the United States, insulted and harassed as a "security risk," and detained within the confines of Ellis Island.

The Attorney General and the Immigration Service refused to accord her a hearing, refused to state the reasons for excluding her, and refused to disclose the nature and sources of the evidence against her. When brought into court on a writ of habeas corpus, they refused the information even to the judges. Twice while the case was pending, they tried to defeat the court's jurisdiction by deporting Mrs. Knauff secretly; but, as luck would have it, on each occasion a court order halted the maneuver at the last moment. To support his refusals, the Attorney General pointed to a 1918 statute which, in effect, empowered him to deny an alien a hearing during a period of national emergency whenever he determined that the alien was excludable on the basis of confidential information which he decided to withhold in what he considered the public interest. The conservative majority of the United States Supreme Court held (4 to 3) that the action of the Attorney General was entirely legal under the old 1918 law and that the War Brides Act made no difference. The situation seemed hopeless.

But the United States is more than its machinery of government, and while high-titled officials were busy embarrassing their country, some ordinary citizens were engaged in rescuing it from embarrassment. Day after day, the St. Louis *Post-Dispatch* and the New York *Post* remonstrated vehemently against the injustice to the Knauffs; the House of Representatives adopted a special bill to permit Mrs. Knauff to enter the United States; and thousands of good citizens spoke or wrote their indignant protests. Finally, the volume of public outcry overwhelmed the men of mediocre minds and worse than mediocre methods. They gave way. Ellen Knauff, granted a hearing before an impartial board, was cleared so categorically that even the Attorney General felt constrained to acquiesce. She left Ellis Island for the last time on November 2, 1951—after a shameful ordeal of three years and three months.

Although one might expect the Immigration Service and Attorney General to have acquired a certain humility from the Knauff episode, the next case showed them as callous and arrogant as ever. A man by the name of Ignatz Mezei migrated lawfully to the United States in 1923 and lived in Buffalo as a law-abiding resident alien for twenty-five years. In 1948 he went to Europe to visit his dying mother. When Mezei sailed back to the United States in February, 1950, holding a quota immigration visa issued by the American consul in Budapest, the Attorney General, acting again on "confidential information," directed that he be held at Ellis Island, be excluded from the United States, and be denied a hearing. During the next two years, Mezei tried to find some other country that would accept him after the United States had stamped him a "security risk." Understandably, with such a label no one would. He sailed twice to Europe, only to be refused by France, Great Britain, and Hungary; he also applied to a dozen different Latin-American countries without avail. His wife and home were in Buffalo; he was free to pace up and down on Ellis Island. Eventually his plight, like Ellen Knauff's, reached the United States Supreme Court.

Ominously enough, the Court's majority opinion (5 to 4) was rendered by Justice Tom Clark. With calm unconcern, it brushed aside Mezei's twenty-five years of lawful and law-abiding residence in the United States, belittled his state of confinement, and coolly sent him back to Ellis Island—there to remain for an indefinite time and perhaps for life. The four dissenting justices—Black, Douglas, Jackson, and Frankfurter—protested bitterly, caustically, eloquently and, it seemed, vainly.

Once again, neither the Attorney General nor the Supreme Court provided the final chapter. *Commonweal* (a Catholic magazine attached to civil liberties), the New York *Post*, and other journals disseminated the views of the dissenting justices. (Dissenting opinions are usually defended on the ground that they contribute to the long-term improvement of rules of law; actually, they do much more. On many an important occasion they notify the legislative and executive branches and, above all, the press and general public that government officials are engaged in committing some immediate act of wrong. Often it is the dissents that awaken, inform, and gird the public sense of injustice.) Here too as in the Knauff case, the American Civil Liberties Union, a voluntary association, helped to spread the alarm. By August, 1954, citizen clamor had reached such proportions that Mezei was released on parole and allowed to return to his home. He had been held on Ellis Island without a hearing for four and a half long years.

Suppose now that we treat the Knauff and Mezei cases as our concrete examples. Before proceeding with the seven questions, let me emphasize that since what we are making is a *Self*-Search, no one can presume to dictate a series of answers for his neighbors' consciences to use; that the replies we may suggest here are only moral generalities, not universal formulas; and that, however an individual citizen may come to judge himself—whether wholly innocent, doubtfully innocent, or clearly implicated—he should never forget that the offending officers of government and their anonymous informers were the guilty principals and that he was, at worst, an accessory in the misdeed. Accessory guilt, serious though it is, should not make one lose sight of the principal culprits.

*First Question (Inciting the wrong).* The citizen's answer is, "Innocent." Exceptions: Newspaper publishers, journalists, politicians, association leaders, and ordinary citizens who during the period of these cases fomented a contemptuous attitude toward civil liberties and fair procedures. A citizen who never heard of Ellen Knauff or Ignatz Mezei was nevertheless an accessory if he urged the government to deny fair play to aliens and persons suspected of subversive activities.

*Second Question (Authorizing the wrong).* The reply is, "Innocent." The responsibility we are assessing here is strictly personal and individual. Consequently, every citizen is exonerated who took no overt action to authorize the exclusion and confinement of human beings without a hearing. The old 1918 statute did not stem from us as individuals. True, it was held to provide the Attorney General with justification in law; but it certainly provided no justification in conscience. Whatever it might imply in terms of collective default and collective responsibility of the whole people, it did not contaminate the citizens as individuals. Exceptions: Those still living who urged the adoption of the 1918 statute, and those who, enflamed with the fever of McCarthyism, supported a new Act of Congress in 1952 which aggravated the situation by converting the 1918 "emergency" clause into a fixed and regular provision of our immigration law.

*Third Question (Installing a conspicuously dangerous instrument).* Here we may say unhesitatingly, "Innocent." There was nothing in the prelude of the two situations to alert us. We received no notice that the heads of the Immigration Service and Department of Justice were disposed to violate accepted national traditions of fair play. Under our system, the officers responsible for the administration of our immigration laws are not elected by the people but appointed.

What the Knauff and Mezei cases revealed indelibly was the dangerous character of the clause under which the Attorney General acted. Before the decisions the danger was obscure; since them it is known and conspicuous. We can no longer disavow the words in the statute book. Yet here again, the duty to reform the legislation is collective, not individual.

*Fourth Question (Failing to prevent the wrong).* The answer depends largely on the specific circumstances of individual citizens. Millions of Americans have never heard of the Knauff and Mezei cases; they can safely reply, "Innocent" here (though some of them have already been implicated by their answers to the First Question). What shall one say of those who did know about one case or the other and nevertheless uttered no protest? Some of them were simply indifferent; some were too busy with selfish affairs; some were too busy with other altruistic affairs; some, splendid with inward resolves, were worthless with pen and paper; some were accustomed to delegate all civic duties to a husband or a father; and some, in the frenetic years of McCarthyism, were afraid to be known as critics of established authority, "malcontents," or "troublemakers." All of them, that is, all who knew about the cases and nevertheless remained silent, may be left to scan their own memories and recall their own motives, worthy or unworthy.

Since a citizen can scarcely be expected to devote every waking hour to opposing the misdeeds of government, he is entitled to concentrate on those that appeal directly to his own competence, vocational skill, personal experience, community interest, and emotional involvement. If he exerts himself to assail a certain list of public injustices, he may fairly assume that other citizens are similarly engaged with their own lists. It is not incumbent on any man to right all wrongs. In general, therefore, when a specific injustice comes to a citizen's notice, he acquires positive merit if he tries to prevent it but does not necessarily default in duty or automatically become an accessory to wrong if he fails to. Of course, silence itself may be guilty—if one internally applauds the act of wrong.

*Fifth Question (Ratifying the wrong).* "Innocent" is the proper answer. Exceptions: Anonymous informers, and all persons, whether now or formerly in government employ or the armed forces, who hide their errors under a cloak of purported "public interest."

*Sixth Question (Suppressing the truth).* "Innocent" again. Exceptions: The numerous respectable and influential newspapers that printed little or no information about the Knauff and Mezei cases even after the facts became notorious. To the extent that jealousy of the St. Louis *Post-Dispatch* and the New York *Post* was a motive for the silence, it was a most disreputable one. If more editors had denounced the Knauff episode, they might have spared us the embarrassment of Mezei's case. Though like individual citizens newspapers are not morally obliged to attack every single instance of official injustice, yet unlike individual citizens they are bound to inform their readers when injustice becomes notorious. Particularly does this become their duty when, as in the Knauff and Mezei cases, the essence of the wrong consists in an official's absolute refusal to account for his actions. By burying the truth, the press makes itself an accessory after the fact. Worse still, it invites a future train of similar official oppressions.

*Seventh Question (Making the victim more vulnerable).* "Innocent" is our reply. Inasmuch as Mrs. Knauff and Mezei were denied admission to the country and detained at Ellis Island, we had no opportunity to increase their personal vulnerability. (But some of us should refer again to the First Question.)

Have we finished now with the Knauff and Mezei cases? Not quite, I think. In posing the questions of the Self-Search, it was only *individual* responsibility we were testing. How, therefore, can we leave the cases without turning once more to our *collective* responsibility? Since the immigration law contains such dangerous provisions, we cannot rest content with a verdict of strictly individual innocence. Our collective default will not be cured until Congress rectifies the immigration statute, forbids the Attorney General to imprison human beings unheard, and thus gives permanent assurance that there will be no more Knauff and Mezei cases. For our motto in the cause of reform, we may choose Justice Hugo Black's wrathful comment on the Mezei case: "No society is free where government makes one person's liberty depend upon the arbitrary will of another." It is high time for the people of the United States to emancipate their immigration law.

This, then, is a working example of the Self-Search and the responsibilities, individual and collective, which it defines and discloses in action.

# V

# *Withdrawal and Association*

## *Responsibility and Withdrawal*

Ever since Chapter I, when we began with the case of Joe and his friend Ted, it has become increasingly apparent that the moral implications of citizenship are not always comfortable and that representative government may entail accessory guilts which no one will welcome. Conducting a thorough self-search along the lines we have marked is at best a disturbing experience, at worst a severe ordeal, and in any event an omen of emergent duties in prospect. A democratic citizen reaches confidently for the fruits of his freedom, and what does he grasp but a fistful of carking anxieties! In dismay, he may come to feel that the whole system has somehow duped him.

"If this," he protests, "is what being a citizen implies, then democracy is far too rigorous for me. The forum of conscience may offer a splendid setting for occasional consultations and debates, but I never expected to reside there continuously. Who am I—one isolated individual in a population of 180 millions—to risk involvement in wrongs and injustices with which I have no real connection? The country is too huge, the administration too remote, the officials too powerful, and—to be entirely candid—I am too busy with my private affairs. Even James Madison conceded that 'The more extensive a country, the more insignificant is each individual in his own eyes. This may be unfavorable to liberty.' That was in Madison's time. Nowadays a single state may have a larger population than the whole country possessed then. Yet you still think it reasonable to lay this burden at my small door?

"Perhaps I should resent the position less," he continues, "if democracy could boast a more respectable history or if the common people knew how to retain their emotional equilibrium. But periodically, if one is sensitive to the higher social values, he is bound to feel—as Plato said in *The Republic*—'like a man fallen among wild beasts' or 'like one who, in the storm of dust and sleet which the driving wind hurries along, retires under the shelter of a wall.' You know how tempestuously the Athenians conducted their affairs. Why, one could form the world's most brilliant community by simply assembling Socrates, Themistocles, Aristides, Xenophon, Thucydides, Euripides, Aristotle, and all the other geniuses whom Athens, democratic Athens, executed or ostracized or drove into exile! As for the modern American scene, can anything better be said—with its frenzied anxieties over 'subversive activity' and 'national security'? Is this democratic government of yours worthy of implicating me involuntarily in its wrongs?

"In the Federal Union there are fifty states now instead of the original thirteen, fifty of them sprawling from Maine to Hawaii across a continent and an ocean. What am I, one helpless citizen, to do? Yes, I appreciate that the federal system was designed for the purpose of preserving the individual state as a governmental unit which would not be too large for citizens to understand and perhaps to influence. Federalism, I know, was invented as a cure for excess of size and population. A seductive theory, this federalism; but what does it signify in application?

"Take, for example, the institution which I personally consider the very worst in American life—I refer to the government's practice of murdering human beings, which you may prefer to call, more daintily, 'capital punishment.' Almost two thousand years have passed since the best minds of Judaism and Christianity rejected and denounced this business of deliberate official killing; almost four hundred years since Chief Justice Coke attested that capital punishment failed to prevent crimes; two hundred years since Beccaria's *On Crimes and Punishments* convinced the leaders of the Age of Reason that capital punishment was irrational, vindictive, and brutalizing. And what has been the outcome? While it is true that certain democratic countries have abolished the death penalty, consider the instance of democratic France, which retains it and still employs the barbarous guillotine. Consider the instance of democratic England, which debated the subject endlessly and continued to hang people while it debated—until at last it abolished capital punishment (almost but not entirely) as late as 1957. Consider democratic Israel, which renounces the infliction of capital punishment—except, forsooth, in cases of treason, which, as all history proves, are the likeliest cases for impassioned prosecutions and unjust executions. And what of America? Each of the other democracies, being governed by a single parliament, needed only a single representative majority to abolish the national disgrace, while in the United States there are no less than fifty state legislatures and the federal Congress for us to cope with. Ought one not feel discouraged? Though the American movement against the death penalty is slightly older than the Republic itself, all except a very few states (about six at present) persist in inflicting it. If it required a century and a half of continual effort to move the British Parliament on the subject, how long will it require to persuade the legislature of, say, Mississippi?

"Meanwhile, I propose to follow Henry David Thoreau's path and withdraw from the whole unworthy scene. If the officials must continue killing people in the name of law, they will no longer implicate me, for I will cut myself off from their brutalities, renounce a franchise that involves me in guilt, and retire to the 'Walden' of my private business (or, as the case may be, my studio, laboratory, library, workshed, card table, or golf course)."

Let us respond in a spirit of candor by granting that much of the complaint we have just heard is valid, whether when applied to ancient Athens, for which we do not feel deeply accountable, or to contemporary America, for which we do. If we would reason profitably with the complainer, we must first undertake to regard his grievances seriously. We must also avoid the temptation to expatiate on the horrors and holocausts committed by despotisms throughout human history and contrast them with the lesser wrongs for which democratic regimes are chargeable. We know despotisms have been and are monstrously worse, but that is a sad sort of defense for democratic government.

On the other hand, it would not be unfair to ask that our complainer turn to Charles Dickens' novels or some other easy source and then consider how many of democracy's own offenses and social evils have been remedied during the past three or four generations. For example, he might consider the drastic reduction in child labor or even in the statistics of capital punishment, which he assails as the worst of our current legal practices. It might also be fair to notice the almost complete disappearance of lynchings. And after mentioning these items, we might go on to suggest that had he lived in Dickens' time, he might have found other legal practices even more vicious than capital punishment. Perhaps the main reason why he ranks it worst is that so many other evils have been abolished.

At any rate, our complainer's outburst does serve to underscore the need for less of haziness and more of clear thinking on the subject of civic responsibility. He has reacted to our analysis by threatening to thrust democratic life away instead of examining it. If he would pause and deliberate rationally, he would see that by sheer dint of defining a citizen's accessory guilts, the analysis has served to confine, limit, and restrict them. Precision cuts both ways. By showing when and how one does implicate himself in an act of official wrong, we have likewise shown when and how one does not. Thus we have offered a measure of reason and clarity in place of vague and disturbing presentiments of contagious guilt.

Let us continue to insist on reason and clarity. If our complainer clings to the hope that by fleeing the political scene he can somehow avoid the contamination of guilt, he is grossly mistaken. All he can accomplish by withdrawal is to make it more certain that his tax money will be used in a way he abhors, that it will continue to pay for the rope, the electric current, the lethal gas, and the uniformed arm that pulls the lever. By like token, if ancient Achilles had not sat sulking in his tent, his friend Patroclus would probably not have been killed.

Why was it possible in the end to vindicate our acquaintances Joe and Ted and secure their lawful release? Because, though capital punishment still remained on the statute books of the state, they had not been sentenced to death but to a penitentiary term. In a "death penalty" jurisdiction, Joe and Ted remained alive to be exonerated. Perhaps this implies that there are incidental gains to be won on behalf of justice and humanity even while we are besieging the main citadel of the law's death penalty: the gain of influencing judges and juries not to impose the penalty where it is authorized but not required by existing law; the gain of meticulous review of capital cases in appellate courts; the gain of inducing governors to commute more and more death sentences to life imprisonment; and the priceless gain of enhancing universal respect for a defendant's right to honest testimony and fair trial. On the long, hard road that leads to total abolition, there are lives being saved and other lives that can be saved if abolitionists do not lose heart.

Yet our complainer is at least partly right when he points to certain practical disadvantages of living under a federal system—fifty-one different legislatures to persuade on the subject of capital punishment. It would be hypocritical to disregard this criticism or predict some early change of the penal law in a state like Mississippi. But, right though the argument is, it ought to be understood consistently. While the federal system does remove a citizen's opportunity to change the statutes of other jurisdictions, it certainly affords him much greater authority to work for abolition within his own state, and thus to erect a moral standard that others may decide to emulate. Recently the State of Delaware enacted a law abolishing the death penalty; it did not have to wait until majorities in other parts of the country were persuaded. Under the federal system New York too could advance without first convincing Mississippi.

Whether we choose or not, the truth is that a man's civic responsibility in the electoral condition follows him wherever he goes and becomes an integral function of his personality. True, there are exceptions to the rule, for some few citizens in a democratic society do seem able to remain in a sort of apolitical womb, sealed off there, ignorant of public affairs, and impervious to the demands of citizenship; I mean certain mathematicians, physicists, musicians, artists, illiterate laborers, and a considerable number of smug housewives. Even such people are occasionally troubled by repercussions of what occurs on the outside and some of them are impelled to emerge. But our complainer, far from being one of the isolated group, is rather more susceptible and better informed than the average; his very complaint demonstrates how familiar he is with the methods and vagaries of popular government and how irretrievably he has lost his pristine political innocence. Whether he wishes or not, he has become a "watchman" like the majority of us, and a watchman he is required to remain.

Yet once he understands the role of a watchman he may be disposed to accept it not merely with resignation but even with some degree of satisfaction. It gives him a place in a very old and honorable tradition, which claims certain preeminent examples in American history. The watchman, in short, is the citizen who descries an evil or a danger and does what he can to warn or admonish his fellow citizens so that they may overcome the evil or avert the danger. By delivering the warning, he discharges himself of the burden of responsibility and shifts it to them collectively. The history of the English and American peoples is replete with watchmen's solemn warnings, protests, monitions, resolutions, interpositions, petitions for redress of grievances, and righteous expostulations. In ethical terms, the watchman seems able to exonerate his own conscience more plausibly when he addresses a somewhat rational modern electorate than a capricious absolute monarch like James I, but the quality of the audience is scarcely a factor he can hope to control. His duty is simply to give the warning and reiterate it until it is heeded if it ever is, and his discharge does not depend on his being successful. As the prophet Ezekiel declared:

> When I [i.e., the retributive forces in human destiny] bring the sword upon a land, if the people of the land take a man from among them, and set him for their watchman; if, when he seeth the sword come upon the land, he blow the horn, and warn the people; then whosoever heareth the sound of the horn, and taketh not warning, if the sword come, and take him away, his blood shall be upon him; whereas if he had taken warning, he would have delivered his soul. But if the watchman see the sword come, and blow not the horn, and the people be not warned, and the sword do come, and take any person from among them, he is taken away in his iniquity, but his blood will I require at the watchman's hand.

A good democratic watchman is one who appreciates that he has been taken "from among the people of the land" and therefore cannot be wholly unlike them. Impatient as he may feel with old, established ills, he will not assume that he is so superior to the majority of his neighbors that they will never understand his message. He will not assume that what he sees—or thinks he sees—so very clearly now, they will never learn to see. He remembers how many times in the past some unexpected and almost miraculous event—like the emancipation of India from foreign rule—burst from the political clouds and dazzled the free world with ecstatic light.

In a democracy, the watchman has a special function to perform. Since democratic electorates habitually disregard noble abstract reasoning and lofty theoretical appeals yet react excitedly when a concrete case of injustice confronts them, the watchman must be prepared to make the fullest rational use of every instance of demonstrated wrong. Democratic memories being rather short, he must exploit the drama fully before it is forgotten. All the humanitarian logic that ethical theory can provide is as nothing compared to one visible wrong, one palpable outrage, one innocent man done to death. Dramatizing a man's tragedy in order to protect others from suffering similar wrongs is a way of rendering partial reparation to him.

Now with our erstwhile complainer metamorphosed into the shape of a watchman, it seems only right to assure him that he is still following the steps of Henry David Thoreau. Under a democratic regime, the resistance which Thoreau preached is a species not of withdrawal but of active civic participation. True, he often saw fit to write as though he were quitting the political world, retiring, retreating, withdrawing, but a genuine withdrawal would scarcely have been so articulate. Thoreau reminds one of the classical authors who became famous through their excellence in declaring the worthlessness of fame. He never retired less from the political scene than when he proclaimed his retirement so eloquently. Not for a moment did he intend to remain quiet at Walden and let the militarists and slaveholders pursue their courses in peace; on the contrary, he was much more dangerous to them there than on city streets and lecture platforms. Thoreau understood that the kind of "peace" he brought was really a sword; he called it not "withdrawal" or "flight" but the proud and contumacious name of "Civil Disobedience." He was one of our finest watchmen, and his horn is still heard in the world.

As Thoreau was not alone even in Walden, so too the democratic watchman of any era need not suffer for lack of dedicated companions if he will seek them and call out. No one stands quite alone in a worthy cause. Near him there are seen and unseen companions to lend their support—not only the potential allies and associates of the present, not only the brave predecessors who served the cause in their own time, but also—in imagination at least—the happy regiments of triumphant successors. These together form the company our watchman depends on as he makes his rounds. And sometimes he listens to what Nathaniel Hawthorne called "that sense, or inward prophecy—which a young man had better never have been born than not to have, and a mature man had better die at once than utterly to relinquish—that we are not doomed to creep on forever in the old bad way, but that, this very now, there are the harbingers abroad of a golden era, to be accomplished in his own lifetime."

### *Responsibility and Association*

As everyone knows, withdrawal from civic life is by no means the only course a sensitive and dissatisfied citizen can resort to; it is not even the normal course. Instead, from ancient times, it has been customary for the citizens of a state to join together and form themselves into groups or societies for the fulfillment of common responsibilities and the furtherance of common interests. Association is powerful magic and can be used with shrewd results. The trick is to make another's interest coincide as completely as possible with one's own.

For example, in the reign of King Louis XI of France there lived a certain charlatan who kept himself in a flourishing condition by his impudence and wit, pretending that he could effect miraculous cures of ailments and diseases and that he could read the future infallibly in the position of the stars. Once when he became angry with one of the king's mistresses because she refused to pay his exorbitant charges, he announced that the stars revealed she was destined to die within the next ten days, and to his astonishment that was precisely what the lady proceeded to do. Incensed, Louis XI summoned the astrologer to court and commanded the royal servants to throw him from the window to his death when they should see the king drop a glove. The astrologer came and knelt before the throne, whereupon Louis said: "You pretend that the stars reveal the exact fate of others to you. Now tell me, what do they say will be your own, and precisely how long have you to live?" Without an instant's hesitation or a sign of fear, the charlatan replied: "Sire, I must confess that I do not know how long I have to live. The stars only tell me that I shall die three days before your Majesty." The glove was not dropped.

In the history of democratic institutions, the right to form associations has had a notable but rather checkered career. The Athenians prized it highly, considered it one of the elementary features of their constitution, and attributed its origin to the laws of Solon. According to Aristotle, association—in the family, in friendship, in business, in culture, in the state—was what shaped and defined a human being, what characterized the morphology of his life, and what evoked the greater part of his ethical and political values. When Aristotle's friend and successor as head of the Lyceum, Theophrastus, was expelled from Athens, the decree of expulsion was declared unconstitutional and void a year later (306 B.C.), not as infringing freedom of speech but as violating the fundamental right of association.

By way of contrast, the leaders of the modern Enlightenment, echoing John Locke, regarded associations with suspicion if not downright hostility. To some of them—mainly the Americans—associations implied secret conspiratorial groups such as they themselves had formed against Britain, selfish economic interests, trading monopolies, sectional antagonisms, and divisive conflicts between city folk and farmers, industrialists and merchants, soldiers and civilians. To others—mainly the French—associations implied archaic ecclesiastical corporations, feudal grants, hereditary privileges, and every other institution that might prevent a free citizen from dealing directly with his government. *The Federalist* papers (1787–1788) made associations appear in the unattractive role of "factions" which might continually threaten the stability of the new republic. In 1789 when Madison drafted our Bill of Rights, he was still of this mind, and inserted no mention whatever of a right to associate or form associations. The right of the people "to assemble and to petition the Government for a redress of grievances," which he did declare in the First Amendment, was simply copied from traditional English sources of the preceding century. For American purposes, this kind of humble, hat-in-hand phrasing ("petition the Government," indeed!) was not only archaic, it was unfitting and obsolete. In any case, it was not the language men would adopt who desired to establish an impregnable right of association. As for the leaders of the French Revolution, they were even more determined on having a molecular or monadic citizenry. By the famous Loi Le Chapelier of 1791 which abolished corporate bodies, they hoped to destroy every intermediate power between the individual citizen and the national republic.

With typical wisdom and insight, Madison soon rethought his position on the subject. In 1787–1789 he had told his compatriots that a federal structure could hold the country—even such an enormous country as America—together if "factions" did not increase in strength and pull it apart. The new Constitution was only two years old when Madison apparently began to suspect that federation would not suffice to mortise the people unless it could be reinforced with other techniques of association. He wrote, as though to himself as well as to us, that "the more extensive a country, the more insignificant is each individual in his own eyes. This may be unfavorable to liberty."

Yet he was still seeking to accomplish the desired result without admitting organized associations, parties, or "factions." If federalism was not enough, then he would place his hopes in improved roads, active commerce, a free press, and the travels of elected representatives to and fro through the country, for "Whatever facilitates a general intercourse of sentiments . . . is equivalent to a contraction of territorial limits, and is favorable to liberty, where these may be too extensive."

Very soon (1792), Hamilton's maneuvers and machinations became so aggressive that Madison openly reconciled himself to political associations and parties as "necessary evils" in a republic. A few months later he went still further and resolved the entire dilemma by distinguishing between associations aimed at supporting the republic, which he approved, and associations aimed at destroying it and setting up a monarchy, which he denounced. From that time on, Madison would reserve the word "faction" to refer to political groupings of which he happened to disapprove. By 1794, when the Federalists in Congress launched a virulent attack on the newly formed Democratic Societies (precursors of the Democratic Party), Madison was prepared to rise and answer all strictures against associations. It was in defending the Democratic Societies on the floor of the House that he uttered his most characteristic and fundamental maxim: "If we advert to the nature of republican government, we shall find that the censorial power is in the people over the government, and not in the government over the people." The sentence ought to be inscribed on all government buildings in the United States, in large letters cut clear and deep; in England it would probably be appropriate to use what Charles James Fox told the House of Commons during the same year while debating the same general problem: "The best security for the due maintenance of the constitution is in the strict and incessant vigilance of the people over parliament itself."

By changing his attitude toward associations, Madison adjusted his philosophy not only to the immediate needs of party conflict but also to what would prove a lasting predilection of the American people. As De Tocqueville, Max Weber, Harold Laski, Max Lerner, and other qualified witnesses have attested, Americans are incorrigible joiners. They are always prepared to join some association or other, and if there is none at hand that suits the purpose, they are prepared to organize one. If an American favors wide streets, he will not be content until there is a Wide Street Association; if he likes to bowl or swim, he is likely to feel that he must join a bowlers' society or a swimming club; if he works as a junior assistant tax accountant for a large corporation, he will not rest until he finds the local Junior Assistant Tax Accountants' Association. There are associations suiting the countless needs and caprices of adults and children and bearing the names of almost all the larger mammals and their offspring. Yet this too has its limits, and sooner or later even an American finds that he has to die separately and without benefit of association; but then he really cannot be said to enjoy it.

As we noticed in Chapter II, the course of philosophic movement in a democracy consists in grasping the Given and using it as raw material out of which to fashion the Created, which in due time will become the Given for a succeeding generation of citizens. A written constitution and bill of rights operates as a kind of ongoing documentary Given, furnishing the people, the officials, and particularly the judges with the warrant they need in order to keep government and law fit for new conditions and evolving standards. And it is in this reference that we discover one of the most interesting aspects of the right of association in America. Because it won Madison's adherence three years too late for the purpose, it is not articulated in the text of our Bill of Rights. In short, it lacks the usual documentary Given.

There are other complications to reckon with. The extremely negative policy which the French legislated in 1791 and abandoned early in the nineteenth century was not without a rational basis, for certain types of association can become dangerous agglomerations of power. In the industrial sphere, we have often seen combines and cartels behaving like feudal barons. In the political, we have watched the Ku Klux Klan, the fascist Black Shirts, and the Nazi Stormtroopers defying law and authority in their respective countries. When it meets this kind of challenge, a government must either succumb or assert itself cogently. If the threat comes or is imagined to come from some clandestine foreign source, it is almost certain to provoke reactions of irrational, even hysterical, violence, as when Englishmen feared the Jesuits, Frenchmen the aristocratic *émigrés*, Americans the Communists. (We say nothing about the mass atrocities that occur under totalitarian regimes, for who would be willing to take them or their behavior as a standard of comparison?) For an unequivocal example of respect for the right of association amid circumstances that were genuinely critical, we should have to turn to Madison's own record as President of the United States during the War of 1812. Despite the panic induced by enemy troops on American soil, despite sedition and treason flaring in the New England States, despite the burning down of the White House, Madison held to his principles, stalwartly defended the right to maintain associations even though they might oppose the nation's war effort, and prosecuted only those persons who engaged in overt treasonable acts. Curious it was that destiny should have reserved this unique episode for the man who had commenced by distrusting all "factions."

In popular political mythology the old distrust still continues, though nowadays we are more likely to hear people talking of a "special interest" than a "faction." Special interest is almost always used as a pejorative label, and seems to be particularly expedient when one wishes to explain why he refused a donation to some indisputably beneficent cause or society. Yet, despite the convenience of the usage, it is at bottom unfair and misleading. For, in any candid view of the human scene, which of our interests is not subject to the very same disparagement? In a larger reference, every interest we can conceive is and must be special. The neighborhood is special in the eyes of the city; the city in the eyes of the state; the farmers in the eyes of the aggregate economy; the state and region in the eyes of the nation; the nation in the eyes of the United Nations; and the United Nations in the eyes of mankind. On the terrestrial globe, man himself is only a limited and special interest, though one which he can scarcely be reproached for prizing and preferring. Yet there is no reason to doubt that every other living interest likewise prefers itself. According to the bible of the birds, God made feathered creatures and nothing else on the sixth and final day of creation.

Every interest we know is in some sense a "special interest," and even the stupendous sum-total which we call the present is only a special thrust made by all the past, a special feint made toward all the future. Perhaps it is precisely because God alone transacts the general interest of universal life that His ways often exceed our understanding, which is necessarily suited to the special.

Granting all these considerations as we must, we certainly ought not fall into the error of believing that the general interest and the special interest are unrelated to each other or, worse still, inveterately opposed. The truth is that there are innumerable confluences between them. God would not baffle our imaginations, in point of fact He would not concern us at all, if His ways did not so frequently address human reason, indicate human action, and reinforce human hope. On the political level, there are many effective concomitances to be recognized between what we call general welfare and what we call particular interest. Workers in a union which advances their standards, farmers in a cooperative which preserves their economic parity, bankers in an association which protects sound financial practices, and citizens in a voluntary society which upholds liberty and equality are serving the whole as well as the parts. In short, though there is nothing like a preestablished harmony between the general interest and the particular, though the general occasionally crushes the particular, and though the particular often attempts selfishly to defeat the general, nevertheless general welfare is an impossibility without many particular, partial, and special welfares.

Hence the dual usefulness of associations in a modern democracy. On the one hand, since our electoral constituencies are established on geographical lines which sweep all the different interests and groups into a single voting district, citizens who desire to advance any special interest or ideal must form an association to give it voice. In this fashion, associations can preserve whatever was really advantageous in the old feudal method of representation (which based constituencies not on geographical lines but on economic and functional classes) without the corresponding disadvantages of inherited privilege and social immobility. On the other hand, associations—by very dint of advocating this or that particular interest—serve to free the elected representative to attend to the more general interests of his constituency and of the nation. In the United States, this by-product is even more valuable because our state boundaries do not follow ethnic or religious lines as boundaries do, more or less, in other federations. Being scattered throughout the Union, our ethnic and religious minorities must depend more directly on their organizations and associations to defend their interests than must, say, the Catholics of Bavaria or Quebec; and by like token our elected representatives are under less necessity to concentrate their exertions on any such restricted interest. In this regard, the American situation tends to resemble that of a unitary democracy like England.

The law of England has recently taken a most propitious turn for citizen associations. Traditionally, English judges insisted that any person involved in a legal controversy must proceed in court on his own initiative and at his own expense and that it was illegal and even criminal for another person or a group to encourage or assist him in bringing or defending a lawsuit. Litigation being very expensive everywhere, and especially in England, this doctrine had the result of defeating many meritorious claims which no one save the wealthy could afford to prosecute. It became more conspicuously oppressive in recent times as an increasing proportion of lawsuits required the offering of expensive expert testimony and scientific evidence. Lately, just such a case came before England's Court of Appeal when a lady who owned land on the river Derwent sued to enjoin an iron company from polluting the river and the defendant retorted that her suit was illegal because it was supported by an association of anglers. Without rudely repudiating the old doctrine, the Court of Appeal restricted it sharply. It held that the interests of the indignant anglers were sufficiently relevant and affected to justify their assistance to the lady in prosecuting her lawsuit.

In the United States Supreme Court, the right of association recently met one of the most dramatic challenges of its history. If law were only a repository of syllogisms as the naïve and ignorant often assume, the right to associate would have succumbed quickly in this instance. For have we not seen that freedom of association was absent from the provisions of our Bill of Rights and lacked a documentary Given? In a mechanical view of law, when the State of Alabama peremptorily directed the NAACP (National Association for the Advancement of Colored People) to reveal the names and addresses of all its members in Alabama, NAACP seemed under compulsion either to abandon its activities in the state or to expose its members to economic reprisals and physical persecutions. Refusing to do either, NAACP appealed to the Supreme Court. There Alabama contended not only that the Constitution conferred no right which would warrant NAACP in refusing the demand but also that if there were such a right, it would necessarily reside in the individual members, who must come forward and disclose themselves if they wished to assert it. Since only natural persons could possess and exercise the fundamental rights of citizens, the State argued that NAACP, being an association, could not plead such rights to defend its refusal. Excellent syllogisms these were, if syllogisms would suffice.

The Supreme Court decided unanimously against the State of Alabama. Many bloody chapters in the history of religious sects, many vital episodes in the emergence of political parties, many economic and cultural values which voluntary groups had brought forth, many intimate ties between group action and the explicit guarantees of free speech and assembly, many practical aspects of what Americans mean when they say "liberty"—all of these stood before the justices and vouched that the right of association was indispensable to the life of a free people. The Court declared that while the Ku Klux Klan could be compelled to disclose its membership list for the purpose of halting its notorious intimidation and violence, the NAACP could not be so compelled for the purpose of merely conveniencing a hostile state administration. And since in this instance the association's members could not come forward personally to claim their constitutional rights without exposing themselves to persecution, the association was warranted in keeping their names secret and speaking on their behalf. In all, the Court wrote a magna carta for the "freedom to associate," declared that any governmental action which might curtail it must be justified under "the closest scrutiny," and created the lacking documentary Given for us and our descendants.

While the law of the subject has grown clearer and firmer, the moral aspect still appears equivocal. Possessing a right to associate is one thing, exercising it with wisdom and virtue is another, which no government is able to assure. Free to act beneficially, associations are also free to act harmfully, foolishly, and viciously. A war veterans' association which agitates for generous treatment of soldiers and their families may also attempt to destroy academic freedom by browbeating educational authorities and publishers of school texts. A religious organization which purifies the reading and entertainment of its members may also seek to impose an insulting censorship on the remainder of the community. A merchants' association which helps to maintain respectable standards of business honesty may also bully the district attorney and the police into prosecuting innocent men and suborning perjured testimony. Voluntary associations of citizens have been known to commit every species of outrage from arson to lynching.

When an association commits a wrong, it incurs the same corporate moral duty to make reparation as any public institution. Obviously, men cannot cover their misbehavior with a cloak of moral immunity by merely forming an association. Yet even the most wicked acts that an organization may commit do not necessarily or automatically contaminate every individual member. For wrongs inflicted by an organization, the member becomes individually guilty under the same circumstances and conditions as a voter does for wrongs inflicted by his public officials. The analogy between them is so close that an association member may use the voter's Self-Search, set forth in the preceding chapter, to determine his individual guilt or innocence. Yet with a somewhat different emphasis, for usually the member's position is not quite identical with the voter's. The member ought to consider that his status in an association is more directly optional than his status in a political community, that his continuing as a member after discovering a misdeed is more apt to signify acquiescence on his part, and that his pleading ignorance of association activities is more likely to sound hypocritical. In short, while the member's Self-Search follows the same general lines as the voter's, the probing ought to be more intense and the outcome more dubious.

There are other moral ambiguities to reckon with. Insofar as a voter's responsibility is moral, no one can delegate it entirely even to the most vigilant and idealistic of associations. If a particular association is engaged in watching the public officials, someone must watch the association, must see that its corporate interests and internal activities do not deflect the members from their main purpose or blunt the edge of their zeal. Mediation of moral duties is all too often a euphemism for dilution. Someone must satisfy himself that long-term objectives are not being sacrificed to the aggrandizement of leaders and permanent personnel. Someone must prevent the association from anticipating those discounts and compromises of its program which will have to be endured in all likelihood when the program passes through councils of the political parties and committees of the legislature, for compromises which begin too close to a measure's source are sure to invite compounded concessions if not total defeat at a later stage. Someone therefore must take care that a libertarian or reform association does not lapse into pleasant accommodation and reasonableness. These continual precautions may make quite a burden for members.

Yet for many reasons the majority of citizens generally find the burden well worth bearing. Assume the case, for example, of an American in the 1850's who abhorred the institution of slavery with all the fervor of his being. To such a man an Abolition Society gave a blessed opportunity to declare his moral faith and repudiate the social evil. Joining its ranks was like nailing the theses of his life to the church door. And this is the way men may feel today when they link themselves with their neighbors to combat some cruel or unjust condition, some enslaving of minds, starving of bodies, or blighting of young lives. The human scene, with all its pain and depravity, suddenly becomes tolerable because membership in an association has provided a chance to take sides.

What are the best associations for citizens to support in a democracy? No one could answer with certitude, but one might say that those associations are truly admirable and excellent in which the citizens, instead of seeking to induce government officials to deal with a social problem, proceed to marshal their own resources, exert their own collaborative efforts, and cope with it themselves.

Obviously, there are many problems that cannot be met in this fashion and that require the application of governmental authority to plan, legislate, and enforce. The government is the community's systematized arm, which should be used whenever its strengths and skills are needed. But it is by no means the only arm; the community has another—the arm of private, direct, unofficial, co-operative endeavor, which should always be kept energetic and supple. It should never be allowed to atrophy.

Voluntary associations could vivify modern democratic society by assuring mobility for men and methods. They could provide room for new ideas to germinate and circulate. They could help to build a truly open community which would continually innovate and grow. It would be the kind of community that welcomed novelty, variety, and spontaneity. It would pulsate with experiments. In it no single manner of doing things would ever be accepted as the final best. Its citizens, far from sitting back and letting problems attack them, would venture forth boldly and hopefully to attack the problems. In all its members, the community would be alert and alive, and it would owe its vitality to free, inventive exercise of the right to associate.

Yet even when the right to associate is employed most honorably and sagaciously, the moral function it can perform is necessarily restricted. There are experiences that do not permit of sharing. At the end of ends, in the inmost of withins, before the ultimate judge, moral guilt remains personal and a man must answer for himself. What democracy does is to challenge the citizens to answer for themselves not diffidently or fractionally but proudly and completely, and as integral men. . . .

Now we are prepared to summarize the responsibilities of our democratic predicament. In the preceding chapters, observing that it was psychologically cruel and politically dangerous for citizens to have no means of judging whether they incurred vicarious guilt when public officials inflicted injuries in their name, we decided to search for criteria which would make the moral involvement more definite and specific. We began by examining the notion that whenever a public officer commits a wrong, he automatically implicates the entire citizenry in his guilt. Finding the notion destructive and false, we rejected it. Then we took the abstract concept of responsibility and resolved it into three concrete active processes, i.e., prevention, reparation, and protest. This step opened the way to the following principles:

*Collective* responsibility in a democracy requires continual demonstrations of prevention, reparation, and protest. Collective responsibility for prevention requires that citizens, property owners, industrialists, and officials develop a solidary sense of community, that they exercise systematic foresight in anticipating social harms, and that they devise public improvements in a spirit of magnanimity. Collective responsibility for reparation requires that citizens and officials punish corrupt prosecutors and policemen for their wrongdoings and, through general state laws, provide adequate means of compensation for their victims. Collective responsibility for protest requires that the citizens, the officials, and the press courageously expose and denounce every official misfeasance and that the state staunchly defend the rights of public discussion, communication, and criticism, no matter how scandalously they may be exercised. Moreover, since all governmental undertakings, experiments, and services are "community enterprises," collective responsibility requires that the state, through general laws, make reparation for injuries inflicted in the course of their operation, regardless of negligence or foreseeability. So much for the performance of collective responsibility.

*Individual* responsibility for official wrongdoing is the moral equivalent of criminal guilt and attaches not only to the principal actors but also to those persons who authorize, incite, assist, or ratify the offense as accessories. No matter how heinous a public wrong may be, it contaminates only the principals and accessories. It never works a universal infection of the citizenry or an inherited infection of their descendants. Each individual citizen can determine his own innocence or guilt by using the questions of the Self-

Search with unsparing honesty. If he feels that citizenship imposes a duty that is unwelcome and onerous, he cannot escape it by attempting to withdraw from civic life. He can discharge his duty by serving as a faithful civic "watchman," and he can share it to a considerable degree by participating in voluntary communal associations. These, despite their practical shortcomings and irreducible moral ambiguities, do provide an opportunity for cooperative exertion in preference to depending on the government. The right to associate is indispensable to the vitality of a democratic nation. If a voluntary association commits an act of wrong, it incurs the characteristic duties of collective responsibility; whether under the circumstances an individual member also incurs moral guilts is to be determined by his intensely applying the questions of the Self-Search. The Self-Search not only specifies moral guilt, it also serves to limit and restrict it. To the humane and decent citizen it offers a rational standard of judgment, a riddance of confusion, and an eventually serene conscience.

# III

# *Displaying the Democratic Incentives*

# VI

# *Equality Passive and Active*

## *Passive Equality*

Here is the point at which we can shift our attention away from moral responsibilities and toward moral incentives. We have examined the negative aspect of our new condition in order to define it, limit it, and thereby render it tolerable. Now we turn to the other side, the positive aspect which renders it not merely tolerable but uniquely and urgently desirable. The moment we do so, we find ourselves in the midst of some of the most ancient and familiar of human experiences. The moral responsibilities that a citizen must bear nowadays may seem novel, but the incentives that make them worth bearing are well known and congenial.

Basic to all ideals of free government is a simple, elementary demand, voiced in one way or another throughout the eras of history: the age-old demand for equality. Equality has a universal appeal, speaking immediately to our ears and understandings—like an orchestra conductor who, with a sweep of one hand, subdues the strings and their subtle frictions while, with a lift of the other hand, he summons the woodwinds, the drums, and the martial brasses. The passion for equality is primordial.

As any literate person understands, when Thomas Jefferson wrote in the American Declaration of Independence that "all men are created equal," he was not seeking to describe men's congenital endowments but their political and legal rights. He was not suggesting that men do not differ from one another in the dimensions and powers of their bodies, minds, and characters; he was declaring rather that, regardless of variations and differences, they all possessed the right to equal political and legal *treatment.* He was not formulating a principle of biological science but a working maxim of public action. The free man's fundamental right is to be treated equally in all political and legal transactions.

This right is incontestable as far as it goes but it does not go nearly far enough; for of what practical value are political and legal equality to a man who has no bread to eat, no clothes to wear, no roof to shelter him, no chance to earn a livelihood? A man must eat before he can discuss public affairs rationally, must have an opportunity for employment under decent conditions for a living wage before he can vote intelligently, and must have a modicum of rest, leisure, and psychic security before he can hold office worthily in a free community. These are the factors involved in what we shall call "passive equality," i.e., the kind of political and legal treatment that preserves a human being's minimum status as a member of society, that keeps him from becoming a beggar, derelict, or outlaw, and that puts a social floor under his deprivations, losses, and fears. This passive species of equality a democratic society owes to all of its members, whether they are citizens or aliens. Consider, for example, the case of Yick Wo.

Yick Wo was born in China and came as a young man to California. Not being eligible for naturalization under American law because he was an Asian, he remained a Chinese subject. For twenty-two years he engaged in the laundry business in San Francisco, always in the same building, under a license from the city's board of fire wardens, certifying that his stoves and irons were safely arranged and did not constitute a fire hazard, and a further license from the city's health office, certifying that the equipment was properly drained and did not constitute a sanitary hazard. Suddenly, after all these years, the city's board of supervisors refused to renew his license to carry on a laundry. They based their refusal on a city ordinance which made it unlawful to carry on a laundry without their consent unless the laundry was located in a building constructed of brick or stone. Yick Wo's laundry was in a wooden building. As he continued to operate his laundry without the supervisors' license, he was prosecuted, convicted, and sent to jail. There he found more than 150 of his countrymen incarcerated on the same charge. Challenging the constitutionality of the city ordinance, Yick Wo appealed to the United States Supreme Court.

It was proved that there were about 320 laundries in San Francisco of which 240 were owned by Chinese. About 310 were constructed out of wood, as, for that matter, were nine-tenths of the houses standing at the time in the city of San Francisco. The supervisors had simply approved all Caucasian applications to conduct laundries in wooden buildings and had denied all Chinese applications. The city attorney argued that the ordinance was equal for all persons because it contained no provision discriminating against aliens or Chinese.

The United States Supreme Court unanimously struck down the ordinance and released Yick Wo and his countrymen. The ordinance, it held, was calculated to subject the laundrymen to the will and caprice of the supervisors, who could arbitrarily deny them the means of earning a living. The Court saw no need to conjecture about the abstract purpose of the enactment, for the history of its application damned it sufficiently. "Though the law be fair on its face and impartial in appearance," the Court said, "yet if it is applied and administered with an evil eye and an unequal hand, so as practically to make unjust and illegal discriminations between persons in similar circumstances, material to their rights, the denial of equal justice is still within the prohibition of the Constitution." Equal words in the law must not be allowed to disguise a deliberate pattern of discriminatory and unequal administration.

This is all the court reports tell us and I suppose all we are likely to know concerning the Yick Wo who won the appeal, emerged from jail, and returned to his laundry. As the law left him at the jail door, so must we. From this point on, we shall be considering a Yick Wo of our own. He will not be an identified individual but a type—a sort of Yick Wo as Everyman.

When he was born in a Chinese river port, Yick Wo required a time to realize that a certain body and its sensations belonged continuously to himself, but as soon as he perceived that his particular "he" was really an "I," he began clamoring on its behalf to possess and master the entire universe. Shortly after, he was taught that his "I" was only a "one," at least in the negative sense that "one does not do such and such an act." Understanding this truth somewhat reluctantly, he came by stages to insist that if his "I" was indeed a "one," then the same principle ought also to apply affirmatively and others ought to treat him equally, as if "each counts for one." In short, he became a normal child.

Evenings he learned to read and write, which eventually gave him a smattering of his people's ancient legends and philosophical aphorisms. During the day, he helped his parents launder the clothes of various rich and noble families. He noticed that though clothes may differ greatly between rich men and poor men, stains and spots and soilings do not. Always studying, he prayed that some day he would become a respected scribe and scholar.

When the river overflowed for the third time in four years, Yick Wo's parents were drowned and he emigrated with his cousins to America. Secretly he dreamed he would be valued there as the extraordinary person he really was, for Americans had announced—had they not?—that they believed in liberty and equality for all men. And how many Americans could possibly know as much as he already knew about Lao-tse or the Analects? It was easy for a man with his advantages to understand why they called their country the land of opportunity. As for him, he must remember not to flaunt his culture or patronize the less fortunate white men; he must conduct himself in a modest and egalitarian style like a genuine democrat. On the ship, Yick Wo wore a good straw hat which had belonged to his uncle and later to his father. Whenever he would admonish himself to meet Americans as though they were his peers, whenever he would renounce his claim of mastery and consent to be treated as no more than equal, he would picture the hat as being doffed with old-fashioned grace and an American hat as sweeping the dust in courtly response.

Let us spare ourselves the ensuing scenes. There is no need to recount the stages in Yick Wo's American education, what wounds, slights, rebuffs, degradations, and insults he suffered, what angers he swallowed, what losses were charged, year by year, against his spirit and pride. For him the instruction may have been particularly bitter because it was so shockingly sudden. Frequently he reviled himself for having approached one more white man hopefully, for having invited one more humiliation.

Yet Yick Wo proved a more extraordinary person than even he had suspected, for after a few years he actually learned to shrug and smile while he ironed the wash. Though they (he no longer thought of the white men as "Americans" but as "they") had passed laws which excluded him and all other Orientals from naturalization, had exploited his labor, had ground him in continuous penury, had forced him to live in a wretched neighborhood and work in a wooden shack, and had reduced a potentially great scholar to a laundryman's existence, nevertheless Yick Wo shrugged to himself and occasionally smiled.

But the arrest when it came overwhelmed him with terror and despair. When he was thrown into jail for merely trying to earn a livelihood, Yick Wo reached the limits of his capacity. If after the other things he had endured they could inflict this final wrong, the world must be wholly lost. At night in the cell he made a solemn agreement with himself that unless he could rediscover some vestige of the America of his earliest dreams, he would have to put a quick end to his suffering and his life. It was on the following morning that he found 150 countrymen within the jail and several hundreds outside clamoring to help him defray the cost of his legal defense. Though the offer bewildered him for a while, he eventually understood the variety of motives that had prompted it.

When the Supreme Court decided in his favor and the case was all over, there was a certain circumstance that Yick Wo could not quite understand. He was never able to fathom, no matter how often he heard it explained, that the United States Supreme Court—the Court that had vindicated his constitutional right to equal treatment —was composed of nine men all of whom were white.

What then of ourselves? It is safe to say that whoever lacks the projective capacity to assume some part of a Yick Wo's experience will never be able to appreciate the meaning of equality. Whoever does not feel the surge of a Yick Wo's resentment and the continual ulceration of his wounded pride is illiterate in democratic values. If there are any human beings so peculiarly privileged that their lives have been exempt from anger and bitterness, the emotional dynamics of a free society will remain as unintelligible to them as a closed book; they have no possible way of reading themselves in. Nor for that matter is it enough for observers to project themselves into a predicament of this kind and sympathize with the sufferings and rages—unless they can also understand how sufferings may degenerate into morbid suspicions and rages into panicky despairs. The demand for equality is no neat diagram devised by a philosopher in the quiet of a study. It is the whole explosive series of human responses to a Yick Wo as he crouches in his cell.

During the three generations that have passed since Yick Wo's time, the social responses to a predicament like his have evolved considerably. The outcome in his case proved to be a landmark for justice, establishing that a statute which might seem to grant equality in formal terms would not satisfy the Constitution if its practical applications were bigoted and unequal. Under the decision, a nation's promise of equality calls for something more substantial, perhaps we should say more sincere, than payment in rhetoric.

In the consumer perspective, what is it that a nation ought to intend when it declares to the world that "all men are created equal"? Unless it is a nation of hypocrites and cynics, surely it will intend: That men are not born equal but are, quite literally, *created* equal; that what creates them equal is not any single force or single event but an entire lifetime of treating and being treated equally;

and that the nation in all its ranks and offices has determined to create living proofs and displays of human equality in action. Construed in this way, the declaration establishes a guiding maxim for every citizen, voter, official, and alien to apply to his daily encounters and transactions.

It may be conceded that the maxim is rather exacting to observe, if only because, as we saw in previous chapters, there is often no effective way to compensate a person who has been treated unequally. In general, it would be unfair merely to reverse the unjust order of the past, say, by giving all Chinese laundrymen a legal precedence over all white laundrymen. For similar reasons, if Yick Wo had starved to death because the supervisors had taken away his livelihood, it would have been scarcely possible to erase the wrong by pushing a number of dollars into the hands of his next of kin. Compensation in cases of the kind will not redress the balance. Hence, a genuine passive equality must depend on society's taking alert measures of prevention, i.e., on its anticipating and obviating the dangers of unequal treatment before the damage can accrue.

The question of livelihood puts us squarely in the realm of economic needs. During the past century, the nations of the democratic world have installed elaborate systems of social security and welfare, ranging from compensation for industrial accidents to subsidized housing, unemployment insurance, old-age pensions, psychiatric care, and national health services. Nowhere are these institutions and services entirely adequate, fixed, or complete. Nevertheless, it is encouraging that the democratic communities have striven to close the gaps in the floor of passive equality and make some sort of provision against the characteristic losses and disasters of human life. And it is good to notice, in the growth of welfare provisions, how the democracies continue to use their social Given as raw material for the fashioning of the social Created, how they persevere in repairing the platform of equality, and how they gradually raise it toward a more dignified scale of subsistence. Most significantly, they have embraced the revolutionary principle that provision for passive equality is not a matter of mere sentimental largesse; on the contrary, it is an accepted public duty and a legitimate personal claim.

Let us return to Yick Wo's predicament and mark some later occurrences. For one thing, we cannot escape recording that various democratic countries are still pursuing harsh and irrational policies toward the aliens whom they admit to their territory. In some instances, aliens may enter on condition, forsooth, that they do no gainful work during their stay; in others, they may enter on condition that they pass humiliating tests concerning their political principles and associations. In each of the democracies, resident aliens are subject to the law's threat of deportation, which hangs over them indefinitely. While these unhappy conditions would seem familiar to Yick Wo, he would probably be delighted to hear the good news of modern welfare legislation and the general inclusion of aliens in its coverage. And he would scarcely believe that Hawaii, on becoming the Union's fiftieth state, had elected citizens of Asian descent to the House of Representatives and Senate of the United States.

Furthermore, Yick Wo may have felt pleased when in 1943 the United States amended its statutes to single out persons born in China from other Orientals and permit them to become naturalized American citizens. Pleased he may have felt but scarcely elated, for like those Chinese laundrymen who had volunteered to share the expenses of his litigation, the United States was merely expressing in legislation its common interest with a wartime ally, the Republic of China. The moment of authentic pride, when America would rediscover the light of its original faith, was still a few years away. It was not until 1952 that Congress discarded the remnant of bigotry and finally declared: "The right of a person to become a naturalized citizen of the United States shall not be denied or abridged because of race."

### *Active Equality*

As passive equality pertains to the necessities of decent human subsistence in a democratic society, active equality pertains to the opportunities for personal improvement and advancement. As passive equality provides a floor, active equality invites men to raise themselves as far above the floor as their individual capacities permit. The ideal of active equality is particularly relevant during a period of social or economic transformation because it admonishes that the benefits arising from discovery, invention, and general progress shall be made available to all members of the community. In this way, as passive equality seeks to provide limits for men's fears, active equality seeks to remove limits from their hopes.

While America has usually been a follower in establishing public institutions of passive equality, it has characteristically led the world in championing the cause of active equality. From the outset, Europeans conceived of the New World as offering idyllic and boundless opportunities. A man could go there, take what he needed, and build a new home for himself in peace. Once on the spacious new continent, he would consider the horizontal boundaries of Europe's provinces and principalities as petty and unimportant as the vertical boundaries of her hereditary class structure. It was a place where he could escape cringing to haughty monopolies, caste privileges, restrictive regulations of the guilds, and royal caprices. Pondering Europe's burden of inherited errors and the freshness of the New World, Goethe remarked, "Amerika, du hast es besser."

Despite everything that has happened since, despite the appearance in nineteenth century America of some of the worst industrial conditions of the old continent, despite the relatively complete closing of the land frontier in the twentieth century, the nation's faith in active equality has remained more or less intact. The people still distrust the very notion of monopoly; where other democratic governments have tended to foster cartels, the American policy, however sporadic, shifting, and self-contradictory, still emphasizes the necessity of policing or dissolving them. Perhaps the most significant aspect of this faith is its hostility to any proposal that looks to mere leveling down. While the typical American, like the typical citizen of other democracies, resents the sight of an undeserved special privilege, he exerts himself not so much to destroy the privilege as to participate in enjoying it. That is why in American experience what begins as a special privilege often becomes first a general privilege, then a general social right, and ultimately an individual legal right. These, for example, were the successive stages through which the opportunity to obtain an education has passed during the course of recent generations. It began largely as a privilege for the more prosperous few, and at last became an acknowledged right for all and each.

What then shall we say of the status of Negroes in America? Some non-Americans may wonder whether Goethe was not mistaken and whether the American Eden was not cursed from the beginning with the reptile of racial antagonism. Some Americans may counter by asking whether our present analysis must continually revert to problems of race relations and whether there are no wrongs and inequalities in America except those inflicted on Negroes. Comments like these, which can be proffered from either side on the best of motives, deserve some sort of consideration. To non-Americans, it is enough to explain that every country has its distinctive touchstone of active equality and that race relations happens to be America's. In other democratic countries, the touchstone will usually be different; it may consist of distinctions of hereditary caste, distinctions of sex, disproportionateness in the distribution of money, the rigorousness of institutional rules and traditions, the irrationalities of class structure, the property-tenure system, the intolerant attitude toward various ethnic practices and attributes, the elastic or sclerotic condition of the industrial economy, or—as history so often attests—the relative status of approved and disapproved religious sects. Much depends on the local touchstone; for example, many Americans would indignantly and violently resist the setting up of an established church, which citizens in certain other democracies seem disposed to accept as a matter of course. Comparisons between one national outlook and another are likely to provoke resentment, and we may properly leave it to our readers to identify the specific touchstones of equality in their respective countries. As far as Americans are concerned, there is only one candid course to follow.

We have to acknowledge that while all sorts of wrongs, injustices, and inequalities are committed in this country that do not involve Negroes (was not Joe's case in Chapter I a noteworthy instance?), it is the evolving status of the Negro that has furnished the main theme for America's saga of equality. And although a great deal has been written on the subject of Negro rights, much remains to be said—because the history is still unfolding and the meaning is still incomplete.

In one sense or another, the whole process has implied a cumulative civilizing of the American people; by precept and example they have been educating themselves in the graduated curriculum of equality. I suppose there was reason from the start to prognosticate that the rate of progress would be cruelly slow. The people have not lacked good teachers of racial equality, but teachers alone would scarcely suffice. It is of the essence of education that many things must be learned that cannot possibly be taught. What the majority of white Americans had to learn—that differences of race have no more proper bearing on personal status than differences of complexion within the same race—they have affirmed at times and denied at others with almost equal fervor, and if it had not been for the courage of the United States Supreme Court, they might still be muddling along with the conditions of the beginning of the century, when racial segregation was the rule throughout the South and in several Northern states. The majority of whites could have learned the import of equality from the holocaust of the Civil War, but they did not. They had a further dramatic opportunity to learn it when the United States entered World War I and great numbers of Negro soldiers served in defense of the country. In those days, the Supreme Court at least drew the obvious inference; it decided unanimously in 1917 that a Louisville, Kentucky, ordinance prescribing segregated areas of the city in which whites and Negroes must respectively reside was unconstitutional. But otherwise, despite sporadic advances for Negroes and militant agitation for their rights, the law and the public attitude remained ambiguous until World War II.

The experience and aftermath of World War II blazoned a new lesson about active equality. It was seen that the bringing together of persons from disparate groups, not for a single, passing transaction but for continuous and ongoing relationships—for example, the relationships arising out of employment—often required a preparatory program of explanation and edification among the affected individuals. It involved recognizing that the hope of achieving their voluntary cooperation was worth a certain measure of waiting and persuading. These insights were provided with a basis in law. During the postwar years, American states and cities discovered that they could gradually attach a community sanction of shame to religious and racial prejudices, and thus make good use of the very conformism we so often lament in our national mores. They found that if the law made religious and racial discrimination punishable by fine or imprisonment, persuasion would be efficacious and prosecution would be unnecessary in the overwhelming majority of instances. Except in the South, almost all the populous states and municipalities having religious or racial minorities installed official commissions to combat discrimination in employment. Through the efforts of these commissions, employers began generally to assume that outright discrimination on religious or racial grounds was no longer respectable.

There was another factor to consider. It became apparent that if employment discrimination against Negroes was attacked as a separate and isolated problem, it would never be solved. Suppose the employers did agree to discard their prejudices and hire qualified workers regardless of race; what would be gained if there were no Negroes qualified to apply for the jobs? Where was a Negro to acquire the training and skills he needed for fair competition on the economic scene? It became evident that equality in employment would remain unattainable in practice as long as there was a gross inequality between the races in educational opportunities. From whatever angle the Negro approached his problem, he discovered that nothing substantial could be achieved without obtaining access to the same schooling as the rest of the population. All his rights, he saw, ultimately revolved around this right. For him this was an important perception. In fact, the future historian of our era may well remark that out of racial segregation with all its cruelty, waste, and wickedness, there did emerge a single incidental good. Goaded by injustice, the American Negro began to appreciate the worth of education, to fight courageously for it, and to pay the necessary cost not only through patience under insult but also through hard and persevering study.

What will the future historian set down when he comes to explain the Supreme Court's Desegregation Decisions of 1954? What will he designate as the proximate causes of these momentous determinations? Our present interest in the 1954 decisions is of much the same order as his; we too are seeking to understand them as specimens of growth and advance in the idea of equality. The data we have are brief and simple. We know positively that, until the end of the 1940's, state laws establishing one set of public schools for white pupils and a separate, ostensibly equal set of schools for colored pupils were considered permissible under the Constitution and that, until that time, the Supreme Court had limited the so-called "separate but equal" systems in only one slight respect. In a 1938 case brought by a Missouri Negro who wished to study law, the Court had held that since the State of Missouri maintained no law school whatever for Negroes, it must admit him to its law school for whites and could not discharge its obligation by merely offering him a legal education in some other state at Missouri's expense. This decision, progressive as it was, seemed rather irrelevant to the situation of Negro public-school pupils, who, even in the most bigoted states, did have a local school of their own, though generally a very poor one. Any state that offered parallel and substantially "equal" facilities on every educational level could presumably escape the application of the Missouri holding. Yet, in its historic action of 1954, the Supreme Court struck down the entire structure of "separate but equal" as unconstitutional everywhere. What had happened between the end of the 1940's and 1954 that prompted the Court to overturn the familiar educational practices of an extensive region?

Let us recognize at the outset that the factors impelling the nine justices were multiple, varied, and complex, that certain justices had always abhorred racial segregation as fervently as Justice John Marshall Harlan did when he filed his lonesome dissenting opinion against "separate but equal" in 1896, that certain other justices seemed to feel no strong intellectual or moral commitment on the subject, and that American public opinion, though hard to measure, tended increasingly to oppose segregation. The factor we are seeking is not what moved the justices as individuals but what moved them as a Court. While segregation was undoubtedly embarrassing to America's foreign relations, the Supreme Court certainly had no authority or responsibility in that sphere. How little those in direct charge of foreign relations, President Eisenhower and the dominant forces in Congress, really desired the 1954 decisions they showed repeatedly during the ensuing years by various inexcusable executive and legislative defaults in implementing the Court's decrees.

For a brief period after 1954, the impression prevailed that it was the expert testimony and scientific writings of various social psychologists that had convinced the Court of the evils of segregated education and had furnished the basis for the Desegregation Decisions. Scholarly analysis soon proved that the impression was mistaken. With due respect to the social psychologists and their propagandistic achievements, it was shown that the Court had relied no more on their views in 1954 than Justice Harlan had when he dissented from "separate but equal" in 1896. Furthermore, when their purportedly scientific tests and procedures were examined, it became manifest that they did not possess nearly enough probative value to warrant a court in relying on them. All one can say about the procedures in the testimony of the social psychologists is that they were probably better than those in the following story, which Professor Herbert W. Schneider of Columbia tells about John Dewey:

I remember once when Dewey was presiding at an educational evening in Teachers College, there was a series of papers on mental testing. And it was all on norms and so on. And at the end of the meeting—I have to tell this story just for the record—at the end of the evening he said, "Listening to these papers I was reminded of the way we used to weigh hogs on the farm. We would put a plank in between the rails of the fence, put the hog on one end of the plank and then pile the other end of the plank with rocks until the rocks balanced the hog. Then we took the hog off; and then we *guessed* the weight of the *rocks!*"

If not the testimony of the scientists, then what did precipitate the decisions? I suggest that, in order to identify the catalyst, one must first recognize a certain elementary principle about the nature of the judicial process and the requirements of effective advocacy. That is, if you wish a judge to overturn a settled and established rule of law, you must convince both his mind and his emotions, which together in indissociable blend constitute his sense of injustice. You must satisfy his mind not only that the general doctrines of the past are wrong in their specific current application but also that they themselves contain, if properly reinterpreted, the guides that will lead to a rule which is right and just. His mind must see not only that the law has erred but also that the law itself proffers a remedy. Then he can feel free to correct the error without betraying the consistency and continuity of the legal order because he will only be replacing mistaken law with correct law. And all this he may determine to do—if you are able to arouse the propulsive force in his sense of injustice, i.e., the excitement of glands and emotions that any man may experience when he witnesses the inflicting of injustice. To achieve a massive change either in law or personal conviction, you must summon both reason and empathy to your cause.

Accordingly, we need to find two more or less concomitant precipitating causes of the 1954 decisions—one which addressed the judges' minds, the other which addressed their emotions, and the former must have indicated some rational way to discard the old rule (of racial segregation) without violating the coherence and continuity of the legal system. This concomitant causation, I suggest, was precisely what took place in two appeals that were argued together and decided by the Court on the same day in the spring of 1950. I think it was these cases that educated the Court to a new level in the curriculum of active equality, and, if my conjecture is tenable, they offer a momentous object lesson in the revising and evolving of social values.

The first case came to the Court from Texas. Aware of how the State of Missouri had lost its litigation by failing to provide a separate law school for Negroes, the Texas officials proceeded to set up just such an institution. They contended that the existence of this special law school justified the state in excluding Negroes from the law school of the University of Texas. And since the state had been fairly generous with the new school for Negroes, the contention it made might have seemed plausible to the Court—if the school involved had not happened to be a school of *law*. Law was the only discipline that the judges understood thoroughly, the only one in which each considered himself wiser than any pedagogic expert. Each felt entirely competent to compare the attributes and facilities of the two schools. The Court held unanimously that the schools were not substantially equal because the law school of the University of Texas had a much higher reputation, quality, and influence and because the law school for Negroes would provide no opportunity for a student to consort with whites, whom he must deal with subsequently in many significant relations on becoming a lawyer. "Equal" as a constitutional requirement was held to refer to something more than buildings, books, and dollars; it referred as well to an extensive list of intangible and nonquantifiable factors. It referred specifically to those indispensable social experiences and human relationships that might make the difference between a student's being merely informed and his being educated. Obviously, on this basis, it would be very easy to conclude, as the Court did in 1954, that all segregated education was essentially unequal. Once the intangibles were taken into account, there was a formula available by which to overturn the entire previous system. The intangibles would never be what they ought to be if the school was a segregated school, and thus "separate but equal" could readily be transformed into "separate therefore unequal."

Yet so far I have suggested only how the judges' minds might have been persuaded, and mental states alone could scarcely overcome the inertia and normative prestige attached to the existing system. To understand what finally made things move, we must find what it was that provided the propulsive power of empathy and indignation. This, I believe, came out of the companion case, a litigation from the State of Oklahoma. It seems that a man by the name of G. W. McLaurin, having a Master's degree in Education, wished to pursue his studies and obtain a doctorate at the state university. The university authorities having excluded him on racial grounds, he had obtained a federal court order requiring them to admit him. Whereupon the Oklahoma legislature did not attempt to set up a separate graduate school for Negroes, as Texas had, but enacted instead that Negroes were permitted to attend the state university "upon a segregated basis."

Now, as long as little white children were pictured as playing lightheartedly in their schoolyard and little Negro children as playing lightheartedly in theirs, a judge of less-than-average sensibility could escape feeling outraged by the spectacle of racial segregation. He—this relatively insensitive judge—could develop the habit of segregating the two groups in his own thinking. "They seem happy enough apart," he might reflect, "and though I personally might not have separated them in the first instance, can I hold that what the state has done for so many years is unconstitutional?" He might continue to reason in this fashion as long as he was not compelled somehow to understand the elementary truth that an individual's life in school is only a portion of his total life in society, only a portion during his school years, and thereafter not even a portion. Our hypothetical judge needed a way to learn that classrooms could not be sealed off from the total society which had created them.

These were the truths that suddenly became manifest in the case of G. W. McLaurin. What Oklahoma did in that case was to furnish the Court with a living tableau, an animated epitome of segregation that even the most insensitive could easily comprehend. For unlike other members of his race, McLaurin had not remained conveniently out of sight in his own schoolyard; he had entered the precincts of the white people and had asked to qualify for the highest academic degree in Education. And once within the university, in the name of "Education" and under the orders of the state and its chief educational officers, how was he treated?

He was required to sit apart at a designated desk in an anteroom adjoining the classroom; to sit at a designated desk on the mezzanine floor of the library, but not to use the desks in the regular reading room; and to sit at a designated table and eat at a different time from the other students in the school cafeteria.

The Supreme Court put a brusk halt to these inhuman practices. In the course of its opinion, further particulars were recited: about the rail that was built to surround the place where McLaurin sat, about the sign on it reading "Reserved for Colored," and so on. What a classroom that was for mankind to admire, what a propitious setting for the ideals of graduate education! How neatly it caricatured the whole segregated society; how accurately it symbolized the influences men let in whenever they try meanly to close other men out! To see McLaurin's position there facing the backs of the white students was finally to understand segregation in a consumer perspective and to judge it by what it had done to human beings of both races.

I have suggested that the two cases of 1950 supplied the intellectual and emotive conditions for the Supreme Court's great Desegregation Decisions of 1954, which have launched America on the most ambitious and admirable social enterprise of the twentieth century. Desegregation will eventually penetrate everywhere in the nation's life. It has proceeded too far already for bigotry to reverse the tide.

Nevertheless, desegregation as presently understood is not nearly enough. The next stage of active equality will arrive when the masses of the people realize fully that the United States is a man's country, not a white man's country with certain guaranteed rights for others. As the country does not belong to a single religious sect, nor does it belong to a single racial group. As even the most gracious tolerance does not provide equality in respect of religion, nor does it provide it in respect of race. Conceivably Hawaii's attainment of statehood in the federal Union may mark the beginning of a new age. Sooner or later, on the higher plane of active equality, Americans will resolve that in all their doings and choosings they can acknowledge no "established" race.

### *Between Equality and Liberty*

That kings and subjects, owners and slaves, white men, yellow men, red men, brown men, and black men are all members of the same genus is so indubitable and obvious that anyone can and almost everyone does learn to demand some measure of rightful equality for himself. The simple physiological facts that inspire the perception stare us in the face. They even tell us that the old, pretentious distinction between "white" men and "colored" men is an open and palpable fraud, that people who call themselves "white" are really not white at all but some shade of pink or olive, and therefore that every living person on the surface of the earth is incontrovertibly "colored." If being colored is relevant, then we are all of us colored, as anyone can see who will look and judge for himself. Paper may be white but human beings are not, save possibly a very few albinos.

The physiological equality between men of superior and men of inferior status is more than skin-deep. It continually embarrasses those in the privileged positions. For this reason, some of history's shrewdest rulers—Pericles, for example, in his day and Stalin in his—kept out of the people's sight, appeared in public only on great ceremonial occasions, and transacted most of their business through emissaries. They realized that the populace would never consider them infallible or superhuman once it discovered that hunger and thirst could overcome them, that they would sweat with fear and shiver with cold, and that their bowels might misbehave like anyone else's. For that matter, what price have pomp, dignity, and majesty to a monarch when his testes become urgent and prompt him to act like any other fool? It is the natural and elementary functions of the body and its organs that give the show away and teach the humble masses more than they are supposed to know about their rulers. In ancient Rome, for example, despite the extravagant ceremony and servile adulation which the city mob lavished on Julius Caesar, they were not astonished to see him bleed when he was stabbed.

The same observations apply with equal force between men of different races. In order for pink men (since "white" is untrue, I propose to say "pink" until I find a more accurate name for the hue), yellow men, or brown men to perceive their equality with men of other colors, they need only consult the simplest phenomena of human physiology. The facts and functions speak for themselves and they all intimate equality. This may be one of the reasons why the notion of a "superior race" or so-called "white supremacy" was bound eventually to collapse. Cortez in Mexico, Clive in India, and the rest of the romantic conquerors may have seemed like gods when they first arrived, but they remained too long, and exposed themselves excessively. Once they were replaced by a system of bespangled colonial governors, strutting garrisons, bumbling clerks, and resident wives, it was only a matter of time before the whole outlandish imperial machine was sure to disappear. Sooner or later, all the subject peoples came to learn what the native domestic servants discovered almost from the start. They learned that these redoubtable foreigners were neither divine nor essentially different but were quite human, perplexed, and vulnerable. Once they perceived this, they had only to wait for the right moment. Eventually, in one empire after another throughout the course of history, some fortuitous blunder or natural mischance would punch a hole directly through the papier-mâché screen of imperial myth, and the whole fabric would fall into shreds. Just as the Persian Empire was put in peril as soon as Xenophon's band of Greeks found they could march through the midst of it to the sea, the English Empire in America was jeopardized as early as 1755 when young George Washington witnessed the inveterate military complacency that cost General Braddock his life at the Battle of the Wilderness and would, in due course of years, cost General Burgoyne an entire army at the Battle of Saratoga.

In the twentieth century, the military factors have converged with the political, psychological, and economic to intensify a universal demand for national independence and human equality. It does not matter very much where the men of one country or another have happened to learn about their right to claim an equal status in the world. What signifies is that, on every front of social relations, equality is the banner under which the peoples are marching. It is the dominant aspiration of the age. On every continent, men are seeking to attain equality with others: in nuclear power, military force, industrial capacity, technical education, public housing, consumers' goods, and welfare provisions. Since massive and commensurable items like these are the very ones that governments are able to produce or at least to foster, the demand for equality creates an immediate pressure everywhere for the expansion of government services and facilities. Whether in a particular country the public happens to own the requisite facilities outright or merely furnishes subsidies for them, the progress of equality necessarily calls for increased regulation and official intervention. A government that undertakes to match the social and economic services of rival governments has no choice but to enlarge its resources of personnel, equipment, and money. Authentic civil equality, as distinguished from rhetorical promises in speeches and constitutions, is not inexpensive.

But suppose that leaders of minority groups in a specific area demand a still further species of expenditure on behalf of their cause. Suppose they urge that personal liberty be renounced in some relatively minor degree to the end of safeguarding the social foundations of equality. Suppose, to be specific, they propose legislation making it a criminal offense to publish a statement or picture which portrays "depravity, criminality, unchastity, or lack of virtue of a class of citizens, of any race, color, creed or religion, or exposes them to contempt, derision, or obloquy." They contend that a law of the kind (called a "group libel" law) would prevent bigots and rabble rousers from inciting riots by defaming minority groups. It would protect and reinforce the bases of racial equality. If incidentally it should happen to abridge the freedom of individual expression, the community's gain in civic order, harmony, and equality would be well worth the cost. Deferring to this atttiude, the Illinois state legislature adopted such a law in 1917 and prescribed a maximum fine of $200.

In order to see what a "group libel" law is, one must understand what it is not. It is not a law against causing breach of the peace or against inciting to riot or against forming a mob to perpetrate some sort of violent action. Illinois, like every other state, already had laws of these types on its statute books, and no one questioned their propriety. But a "group libel" law attempts to go much farther; it seeks to control words without immediate or necessary reference to deeds. It attempts to proscribe the implanting of certain vicious ideas and unhealthy mental associations that may or may not engender a resort to violence. Pointing to the sanguinary history of race riots in Illinois, the sponsors of the group-libel law contended that hatred of minorities must be stopped at the source. According to them, the state ought to prohibit calumnious propaganda before it could reach the general population and begin its work of infection.

Shortly after World War II, a bigot by the name of Joseph Beauharnais, convicted for violating the Illinois group-libel law, appealed to the United States Supreme Court on the ground that it was unconstitutional. The record in Beauharnais' case was terse and simple. It contained nothing about violence or breach of the peace. All it showed was that, at a meeting of a so-called White Circle League, he had distributed bundles of a leaflet which, in disgusting terms, defamed the Negroes of Chicago and petitioned the mayor and city council to halt them from encroaching on "white" residential neighborhoods. At his trial in Chicago, Beauharnais had offered to prove that the leaflet's nauseous statements about the Negroes, their rapes and robberies, were factually true, but the judge had rejected the evidence. On this record, the Supreme Court held (5 to 4) that the Illinois group-libel statute and Beauharnais' conviction were constitutional.

Our present concern is not with technical issues of constitutional law but with the basic principles of democratic government. In our perspective, it seems clear that the Illinois statute and the Supreme Court holding were mistaken. Some readers will disapprove of the Court decision as soon as they learn that Beauharnais was not permitted to defend himself by attempting to prove the truth of his statements. They will reason that if he was telling the truth, the social interest in what he had to say would be the same whether he spoke in good faith and for a benevolent purpose or in bad faith and for an abhorrent purpose. Allegations and opinions which may contribute to shaping public policy are not less true and meaningful when they emerge from a vicious mouth. If we cannot trust our electors to discriminate between truth and falsehood, then we cannot say that they are morally responsible. If they are to be deemed responsible for the disposition of public affairs, they alone must decide between social meat and social poison.

Yet could anyone seriously urge that a judge ought to entertain evidence of the kind Beauharnais was offering? Ought a judge allow testimony to be introduced which, whether or not it was believed, might serve to humiliate and degrade a whole segment of the population? Do we desire him (or a jury, as the case may be) to decide whether Beauharnais' insults were true or false in fact? Nothing could be worse to contemplate. Imagine, if you please, a judge who reads in the Illinois statute that groups must not be accused of "lack of virtue" and then, after listening to the evidence on both sides, proceeds to announce a decision concerning the "virtue" or "lack of virtue" of Negroes, Jews, Catholics, Irish, Italians, Poles, or any other social group. Picture, if you like, the submitting of such a question to a jury of laymen, any jury at all! Manifestly, the very notion would be intolerable. We the people have not established courts or juries to pass judgment on the *general* merit of any group among us. Judges and juries cannot vindicate a whole group because they cannot condemn a whole group; their verdict of acquittal would be as impertinent as their verdict of conviction.

Thus, along one path or the other, we encounter a hopeless anomaly in practice. The laws against group libel appear equally unacceptable whether the court admits evidence to support a defense of truth or excludes it; a court is simply not the place to contest and determine issues of wholesale or general desert. The function of a court is to determine particular desert, i.e., the desert attached by law to some specific overt action or some specific incident of default or negligence. A court's business is to assess men's particular transactions, not their over-all human worth, and no secular tribunal possesses the authority to judge an entire social group.

There are larger implications for us to consider. Suppose we test the pragmatic validity of the Illinois group-libel law by assuming that the authorities would apply it quite literally, allow no exceptions, and prosecute every publication which "portrays depravity, criminality, unchastity, or lack of virtue of a class of citizens." The consequences would be interesting indeed. Of course, the state should begin by prosecuting anyone who distributed the Hebrew Bible, which in innumerable passages portrays the depravity of Jews. Then the Gospels might follow in obloquy, if only because they show how Christians failed Jesus in his hour of deepest crisis. Greek literature would be banned for calling the rest of the world "barbarians." Roman authors would suffer because when they were not defaming the Gallic and Teutonic tribes they were denigrating the Italians. The Christian writers of the Middle Ages frequently castigated both Jews and Mohammedans. Dante consigned entire vocations and professions to the Inferno. During and after the Reformation, Catholics and Protestants wrote dreadful things about those whom they reciprocally styled "heretical," an epithet which when properly understood and aggregated comprised the whole population of Christendom. Shakespeare bluntly affronted the French, the Welsh, the Danes, the Calibans of the underdeveloped countries, and sundry important denizens of the fairy kingdom. Dozens of writers from Sheridan and Dickens to Shaw and Joyce insulted the Irish. And surely any author or statesman who ever championed the emancipation of Negro slaves or the equal treatment of Negro citizens had to be guilty of portraying a specific "depravity or lack of virtue" in the dominant majority. Are not they, the pink (white) people, a group too, and entitled to have the sensibilities of a group? If so, then the ban on group libel would attach to almost every item of worth-while prose or poetry which has yet been published by an American Negro!

If the sponsors of group-libel laws are able to regain composure after reading the last paragraph, they may retort: "This literal application is not what we intended, not at all. The judges know quite well that the group-libel law was enacted to protect minorities, not to muzzle them or censor classical literature. We can trust the judges to avert any undesirable consequences. The judges will interpret the statute suitably in each case that comes before them. Depend on the judges!" And here, in this reply of theirs they have unintentionally provided the key to a general maxim about equality and liberty in a democratic society. The maxim is: Whenever zealots attempt to advance civil equality by abridging freedom of thought and expression, they almost invariably defeat and annul their own purpose. For see, please, the paradox that our interlocutors have constructed for themselves. In order to secure what they hope will be a gain in terms of equality, they propose diminishing not only a species of liberty (liberty of expression) but a priceless species of equality itself (equality before the law) as well. They ask not only that we restrict freedom of the press but also that we confide our fates to the unpredictable case-by-case discretion of particular judges and juries. They would have us give every tribunal a sort of roving commission to investigate and decide whether this book, that leaflet, or that picture insults more than it informs, informs more than it insults, or—being extremely ancient and inaccessible to hoi polloi—has acquired an immemorial license to insult with impunity.

Is there such a thing as political equality without liberty? Despite the casuistries in communist and other totalitarian literature, it does not seem possible in concrete human arrangements. If equality means what we have taken it to mean, i.e., the equal treatment of human beings, then a total eradication of liberty, instead of assuring equality, would seem to make it quite impossible. In our sense, two slaves are the most unequal of all persons because neither of them has a right to claim any particular level or standard of treatment. One may be treated generously, the other cruelly; in either case it is all a matter of grace or transient caprice. Because a slave has no right to the continuation of whatever he happens to be enjoying at the moment, he has nothing to present as a measure of stable comparison. Even his subjective feeling of misery must be volatile and discontinuous. Equality in our reference involves an *assured* sharing in official or social goods. It is functionally inseparable from freedom of thought and expression because it subsists not among rightless chattels or identical juristic concepts but among irreducibly unique human beings.

In point of fact, the ideals of equality and liberty are so intimately amalgamated in the transactions of a democratic society that we frequently do not know which of them to invoke. For example, in a number of American states, there is legislation which forbids a person of one race to marry a person of another race. Is this legislation a denial of equality or of liberty? In the context of the American Negroes' struggle to achieve an equal status in all civil relationships, these laws are generally attacked under the rubric of equality. The group resents them as badges of inequality. But ordinarily when two young people fall under the spell of love, they are less interested in a general equality between groups than in a specific liberty to marry whom they please. In their eyes, the laws against intermarriage constitute a cruel and capricious infringement of their personal liberty. Theirs is the more forceful and moving complaint; it accords with our society's basic assumption that, except in cases of infancy or imbecility, the individual ought to be free to choose his matrimonial partner. The state laws against intermarriage are clearly unconstitutional and sooner or later will be struck down by the Supreme Court. For the time being, they illustrate the truth that liberty and equality are often alternative and interdependent facets of the same democratic good.

If this is so, what shall we say to De Tocqueville and his brilliant analysis of the outlook for democratic man? Have not he and his epigoni admonished us for nearly a century and a half that equality on the rise implies a grave probability of liberty on the decline? Equality, we have read, is ordained to prevail everywhere in human affairs, yet at a grievous cost not only in the goods of political freedom but also in the humanistic and social goods, the refining influences, personal excellences, and urbane arts that aristocratic societies of the past were proud to display. We have been told that we are to have men of equality who will embody and generate the interests and traits of the popular mass and who are as likely to lose whatever was meritorious in aristocracy as to gain whatever is meritorious in democracy. Our more recent mentors have been emphatic concerning the losses and unsure concerning the gains. All in all, we have become familiar enough with the outline of the man of equality. What our time requires is a clearer image of the democratic citizen as a man of quality.

# VII

## *Quality: The Virtue of Judgment*

### *The Search for Quality*

What is quality in a democratic order and what do we intend when we call one of our neighbors a citizen of quality? The interest in this subject goes back to the first groping stages of political theory. Following the leads that Socrates and Plato had set for him, Aristotle inquired into it with characteristic sharpness. For the population of his ideal state, he said he preferred Greeks above all other ethnic stocks because their climate and terrain prepared them to excel in the qualities of intelligence and spiritedness, which he considered the most useful and valuable. In the centuries after Aristotle's time, the passages he had written on citizen quality attracted little notice and even less approval. The statesmen of the Roman Empire could scarcely disregard the calamitous military and political decline that had befallen the Greek nation, nor could they welcome the restless questionings that Greek scholars brought with them when they came to teach at Rome. Aristotle had astutely observed that what one desires in citizen quality depends largely on the kind of political constitution one has in mind, and the men of successive eras who subscribed to constitutions of universal empire or feudal lordship or absolute monarchy had no desire to define, much less to encourage, traits and qualities that might befit citizens living in a democracy.

Nevertheless, the inquiry was too important to disappear from political thought. It sprang into prominence again toward the end of the seventeenth century when European travelers returned from China with glowing accounts of the Confucian principles of public administration. With perhaps more enthusiasm than accuracy, they published descriptions of the Chinese system for selecting officials and training them in their duties. The Chinese, they explained, wisely overlooked considerations of birth, rank, and wealth in order to find officers and administrators who possessed genuine personal talent. Soon, for this and other reasons, it became a favorite doctrine of the eighteenth century Enlightenment that government careers—and all other careers—ought to be open to any man of personal talent.

Meanwhile, the cultural leaders in America were growing familiar with the pages of Montesquieu. They found him combining what he had gathered from Aristotle with what he had gathered from the Chinese. Quality, he agreed, did vary according to the nature of the particular national constitution. In a monarchy, one needed honor; in a despotic state, one needed fear; in a republic, one needed virtue. By the time that Thomas Jefferson came to reflect on the subject, "virtues" had been added to "talents" as desiderata, making "virtues and talents" one of the standard democratic slogans. Jefferson declared that the true natural aristocrats in a democratic polity would be the men who excelled in virtues and talents, and though John Adams commented that, in any popular contest, the virtuous and talented would always lose to the well-born, the rich, and the handsome, he declined to retreat from the formula. He merely added, along with virtue and talent as qualifications of a democratic aristocrat, the further attribute of "courage"—which corresponded, one supposes, to "spiritedness" in Aristotle's list and "honor" in Montesquieu's. On this item at least all the sages seem to concur; they all assert that courage or honor is indispensable and that without it neither wisdom nor benevolence will avail as civic qualities.

As for other qualities or virtues, Jefferson said strangely little by way of specification. Which virtues or talents are we to look for? His reticence is uncharacteristic of him and implicitly discouraging for us. Perhaps having contemplated the contingencies and vicissitudes that beset the careers of men and peoples, he despaired of offering any more precise counsel. Perhaps he knew much more than he felt able to communicate. (Political wisdom is rather like a newborn babe, easy and light to hold but difficult to pass to another.) Again, he may have recalled Aristotle's wise admonition that a good state does not attempt to establish any single, uniform pattern for its citizens but, on the contrary, fosters an enriching variety of interests and personalities among them. Finally, it is possible that Jefferson decided to be unspecific because he had resolved to avoid such a pit as Montesquieu had dug for himself. For when Montesquieu began to identify the specific virtues that would befit a republican people, he became so passionately absorbed in the single virtue of frugality that he advocated a rigorous official censorship to regulate the people's habits, expenditures, and living standards. No wonder then that after reading Montesquieu, Jefferson felt satisfied to express generalities!

In the present posture of affairs, our supreme need is for citizens who display quality in *judgment,* quality in *honor* (or courage), and quality in *associability.* These qualities are the indispensable three. If one wishes to fit them into the traditional schema of political theorists, one can say that judgment, being exercised for the most part individually, partakes of the monarchic; that honor, being a product of superior self-esteem, partakes of the aristocratic; and that associability, being a mark of concurrence in popular will, partakes of the mass-democratic. Be that as it may, judgment, honor, and associability are the qualities that determine the fate of a modern democracy.

For candor's sake, let me acknowledge at the outset that in one vital respect I shall diverge from what Aristotle seems to have taught. He seems to have assumed that *all* the desired civic qualities should vary directly with the form of the national constitution, that education should always develop a type of character expressive of the particular state, and that a democratic education should consistently inculcate a "democratic type of character." The principle seems quite correct insofar as it is applied to the quality of associability. I do not doubt that a democratic education ought to prepare a young citizen to accept majority decisions and cooperate willingly with popular enterprises.

But can the same be said with equal force of other personal qualities such as judgment and honor? I believe not. To me it seems arguable that these ought to vary *inversely* with the form of state constitution. I suggest that the more effectual the power of majority rule in a given society, the more acute the social need for independence, originality, and even recalcitrance in the quality of individual judgment. By analogous reasoning, when it is honor that we seek in the public transactions of a democracy, generally we are required to disregard the mediocre standards of the many and apply the superior standards of the few. Thus, the quality of a democratic citizen may display itself most admirably when his judgment opposes the majority and his honor requires him to contradict them to their face.* Without the boon of outspoken dissent, communities tend to become shabby and unfree. Any mode of education that would reduce democratic men to the single attribute of associability—i.e., to acquiescence, conformity, and collaboration—would demote them as free citizens. There are occasions when the only effectual way an honest man can serve his neighbors is to tell them, at whatever cost to himself, that they are altogether in error.

### *Quality in Judgment*

In this age when men are brave to ask divine questions but lack the courage to proffer human answers, when they engross themselves with contriving flawlessness in the laboratory but whine be-

* It may well be that the only real difference between Aristotle's conclusions and mine is that he premised a strictly majoritarian democracy (which I consider neither viable nor desirable) and I premise a majoritarian-libertarian one.

cause they do not find its replica in the street, when they turn dizzily from text to text and fad to intellectual fad, always pursuing some dominant formula or master phrase to which to surrender their freedom—in this age if ever, there is a need for superior quality in civic judgment. The educated people of the West took more than a millennium and a half to recognize that the god who might answer them was not imprisoned within institutionalized theology; then they took two hundred years more to learn that wisdom was not encapsuled for them within the tomes of philosophy; and recently they devoted another century to discovering that ethical and political salvation is not confined within, nor will it ever issue from, the apparatus of science. Though the library and the laboratory yield useful information and desirable skills, a conscientious citizen who comes to the crossroads of decision always finds that he has to judge for himself and assist his neighbors in judging for themselves. Theology, philosophy, and science are only special resources of our society, repositories for particular arts. They offer us hints, precedents, analogies, clues, techniques, subordinate clarifications, and grist for our deliberations. Ultimately, after giving them the fullest deference and attention, we can only exercise our own choice and shoulder the consequences. To elude a choice by parroting what the theologian or the philosopher or the scientist has said is nevertheless to make a choice and an unworthy one. In the shaping of social arrangements, all the vaunted "methods"—scientific, juristic, statistical, analytic, or experimental—can never be more than transitory instances and concrete manifestations of the single authentic method: the method of free intelligence. Without quality of judgment, there is no eventual virtue in any method.

In the main, the classic philosophers have appreciated the importance of good judgment but despaired of developing or cultivating it in their students and readers. Even Immanuel Kant, whom we tend to associate with rather automatic categories and mechanical logic, acknowledged that the best of philosophies would avail little to a person who lacked the gift of judgment. Like most of us, Kant considered judgment a matter of native endowment which could not be supplied by any pattern of training. He noticed, as the rest of us do, how many learned professors behave fatuously and how many uneducated peasants decide wisely when judgment is called for. Perhaps at bottom nature is really more democratic in its distribution of capacities than genetics has been willing to concede.

Is it really impossible to say anything constructive about the training of judgment? If judgment cannot be implanted, may we not suggest how it may be usefully improved? We have the advantage here of concentrating on political and civic affairs. We begin with a specific area of reference. Though the general judgment of a total man may be beyond anyone's capacity to train and cultivate, we may find that much can be done to improve the restricted judgment which is needed for political decisions. How to choose a wife is one matter, how to choose a congressman another, and about the latter we may possibly say something of use. Accordingly we suggest that there are three indispensable factors in the shaping of judgment which a reasonably intelligent and reasonably benevolent citizen can analyze, understand, and learn to employ. Since these factors have a substantial basis in reason, a citizen can practice them consciously, habitually, and progressively. They are: The Use of Due Process in Judgment; The Use of Compassion in Judgment; and The Grading of Belief.

*The Use of Due Process in Judgment.* "Due process," a standard that arose in our system of law and stemmed from the desire to provide rational procedure and fair play, is equally indispensable in every other kind of social or political enterprise. Almost invariably when we fail to employ due process in exercising judgment, we find to our dismay that we have not only inflicted a wrong on someone else but have also harmed ourselves through a destructive blunder. To the human object of a judgment due process affords protection against injustice; to the human subject it affords protection against costly stupidity.

What are the main elements of "due process" in *legal* usage? To begin with, it admonishes that we must not accuse anyone of violating a standard of behavior unless he could have ascertained the existence and meaning of the standard before he took action. We must let him know what he is accused of doing and give him a fair opportunity to collect his evidence and present it. The judge and jury who hear his case must be unbiased and attentive; and, especially where the accusation is a grave one, the accused is entitled to the assistance of a counsel and advocate. Moreover, even after an accused has been found guilty, due process of law requires that we provide some sort of remedial procedure to uncover and correct any serious error that may have been committed in disposing of his case.

It is easy to see how we need the very same steps or their equivalents when we judge men's behavior in *political* life; the respective analogies are obvious enough. But suppose it is not men and their behavior but general principles and conflicting public issues that we are required to judge: will the standard of due process still prove serviceable? I submit that it will. It counsels: that in conducting social inquiries we ought to make certain that our antecedent standards are rational and intelligible; that whenever we encounter a controversy we ought to investigate and consider all the pertinent evidence, however unexpected or contradictory it may be; that we ought to cleanse ourselves of prejudice, narrow partisanship, and improper bias; that we ought to suspend decision until we have attentively assessed the factual records and opposing arguments; and that, remembering the inevitable margin of human fallibility, we ought to be prepared to reconsider our conclusion if at a later date it appears likely that we have erred.

Granted and agreed; but there is one further requirement which the law imposes and which we have not yet translated into the language of political judgment. What shall we say about the legal rule that if an accused lacks an advocate to speak for him, the court must furnish one? Does this too have an equivalent in politics? Evidently it does. Since all human beings—including the soberest judges on the bench—are susceptible to what we may call "the disease of advocacy," a maddening infection that can strip a man of restraint and reason, annul his sense of proportionateness, blind him to the substance of a controversy, depersonalize and dehumanize his adversaries, and drive him headlong down any decline that seems to promise him victory—since such is our generic state, the only way to remedy this weakness of ours is deliberately to match argument and advocate on one side with argument and advocate on the other. Thus it becomes our duty to imagine a faithful advocate on behalf of the opposite side of any question, to accost him and whisper suggestions in his ear, and prod him to do the best he can for his cause. If then he fails, we can conscientiously believe that we have accorded due process to the political controversy. On occasion his plea will surprise us by succeeding. More often, though he may fail, he will persuade us to evaluate the issue more modestly and consider the desirability of compromising.

Why is it imperative that we practice due process? Because experience has taught that every method men have devised for ascertaining the factual truth is materially imperfect. Due process is at once our acknowledgment of ignorance and our device to mitigate the damage that ignorance inflicts. Most of our civic ineptitude comes from not knowing the elementary facts that have to be established before the process of judgment can even begin. When we consult the views of commentators and experts, we discover that they differ from one another for the selfsame reason, i.e., confusion and conflict concerning the elementary facts. Sometimes one wonders whether any two observers are writing about the same man, the same event, or the same controversy. They are like Whig and Tory, Protestant and Catholic, French and German historians who seem to be recording two different Englands, two different Reformations, two different sets of military campaigns.

As Judge Jerome Frank explained in the brilliant critique of fact-finding which he called "fact skepticism," even the most objective and honest witness—how many witnesses can be considered thoroughly honest?—may (1) observe poorly, (2) recollect weakly, and (3) narrate ambiguously—not to mention that by the time the general public receives the story in a book, newspaper, or telecast, the errors, deviations, and distortions have been squared and cubed as each successive transmitter or interpreter displays a new combination of shortcomings in observing what *he* witnessed, recollecting what *he* observed, and relating what *he* recollected. No wonder, then, that in criminal courts the identification testimony of respectable eyewitnesses, which one might assume to be the very acme of reliable evidence, has induced a greater number of guilty verdicts against persons later proved to be innocent than any other source of error!

Even the most conscientious use of due process cannot guarantee a correct judgment in every instance; this much we must acknowledge. But though the thought of our fallibility may sober us, it need not inhibit the exercise of intelligent judgment. If errors are inevitable, we can take precautions to minimize them and limit the sufferings they impose. By questioning, doubting, scanning, and probing as due process requires, we can demonstrate a decent respect for the opinion of our neighbors, the welfare of our country, and the quality of our own acts of judgment. To presume to judge without due process is to sink to the level of the beasts of the field. To employ due process painstakingly and conscientiously and then stand responsible for the outcome is man's true dignity.

*The Use of Compassion in Judgment.* To avoid being misunderstood at the outset of this topic, let me say summarily that I am not about to recommend the use of political sentimentalism. On the contrary, I am convinced that a foolish sentimentalism is as discreditable to compassion as a wooden legalism is to law. Nothing has done more harm to compassion's good repute and rational exercise than the preaching of bathos and the dispensing of emotional treacle. In any society, there are many psychically insecure individuals who actually prefer the government and law to be strict, inflexible, merciless, and even arbitrary; they feel uneasy with a legitimate command unless it requires blind and abject submission of them. They see no relation between compassion and law except the relation one might find between a temporary sedative and an incurable disease. Obviously, this is not the attitude we mean to encourage when we endorse the use of compassion in judgment.

On the contrary, the compassion which interests us, instead of expelling human reason, enlightens it, instead of opposing official law, emolliates it, and instead of nullifying political judgment, pervades and informs it. What we need to develop in modern democracy is neither a judgment without compassion, which is bound to be harsh, nor a compassion without judgment, which is bound to be dangerous, but a continual application and intelligent use of compassion-in-judgment. We need reason and compassion to collaborate with each other and reciprocate their respective merits. A sound democratic judgment would reflect the influence of compassion at the start and at each successive stage of its operations.

Is there any reflective approach that citizens could adopt in order to develop a regular habit of judging compassionately? If there is, it would have great pedagogic value in a democracy. Let me suggest then that, as an experiment in political ethics, we fix our minds temporarily on the following propositions which together constitute a kind of rational preamble to the use of compassion. The phrase may seem a bit incongruous (a *rational* preamble to compassion?), but only because we have been so long controlled by the dualism between a supposedly heartless judgment and a supposedly senseless compassion. If we are to succeed in yoking judgment with compassion, we must first acknowledge that compassion need not be an offspring of impulse or a mere foundling in a reasonable world; we must acknowledge that many sober reflections are available in a rational man's experience to inspire and recommend it. Here are some of the most cogent *rational* incentives toward compassionate judgment:

1. As the insights of fact-skepticism make plain, our knowledge of facts is generally too undependable and imprecise to support any harsh or categorical accusations. We do not understand our own motives thoroughly, much less the feelings and sufferings that may have actuated others. Ought we not be slow to judge and loath to condemn?

2. When a contest draws to its close and reaches its outcome,

the loser's claims may be wholly overwhelmed, although against almost any other contestant than the one he happened to draw they might easily have prevailed. Almost always the loser's cause does not lack merit; it simply falls short before the adversary that fate or chance has thrust on it. Yet life often fails to award a prize for second place, and defeats are likely to be total. Consequently, as Aristotle remarked, an equitable man will try to avoid resorting to strict adjudications which give all to one side or all to the other; if disputes must arise, he will usually prefer to have them adjusted by compromise or arbitration.

3. Time being a dimension of all we feel and know, the man who wins at the end is not the same man who set out in the contest. Inevitably the interval and the effort have modified him. In order to win, he must necessarily lose something of the self that he began with, something of the self that initially deserved to prevail or be vindicated. In the nature of time and struggle, there can be no complete winner.

4. Likewise when the laborious hour of victory does arrive, the very thing that was fought for can be seen to have changed from its original aspect and worth. The prize has passed into something other than it was at the start of the contest. In every literature of the world, one can find some very special lament for men to recite on the occasion of getting and possessing what they once ardently desired.

5. Somewhere in every deed that is aesthetically repulsive, intellectually contemptible, or morally evil, we can identify a trace of sickness. Perhaps the cause has to do with the individual's biological heredity or his social environment; perhaps it has to do with some perverse mischance or farfetched coincidence between an extraordinarily acute desire and an extraordinarily tempting opportunity. The sickness is nonetheless real, though in some instances we can say merely that it is incidental to his being a member of our species. A biologist might put it that the greater part of any person's fitness for survival is not of his own making and has little to do with his earned desert. If the fittest do happen to sur-

vive in the struggle, what does it prove in most instances except that they are the fittest to struggle and survive, yet not by any means the fittest to be approved? Being fit to survive is itself a kind of implicit commentary, never a quite favorable one, on the condition of the survivor's environment.

6. Since everyone is linked and associated in a variety of intimate ways with the lives and destinies of others—parents, spouses, children, friends, co-workers, employees—we find ourselves unable to reward any person at all without conferring a series of corollary benefits on others who may be entirely undeserving. Nor, by like token, are we able to punish any person without a grave probability of harming the innocent ones within his orbit.

7. Granted that mature judgment and seasoned wisdom can scarcely be acquired without undergoing a measure of pain, yet how much superfluous pain there is in all the houses of men, that no one really deserves, that no one can benefit from, that teaches no one anything, that is cruel and wrong beyond defense and even beyond description—and that it would be unthinkable for us needlessly to increase by as much as a single wince!

These are some of the thoughts a citizen may weigh whenever he is required to make an important decision. If he does consider them seriously, his judgment is more likely to exemplify the qualities of modesty, tolerance, equity, and compassion. He will wait and search for the truth, and while searching he will presume innocence rather than guilt, mistake rather than malice, repentance and new effort rather than irremediable wickedness. When at last he comes to judge—as every citizen frequently must—he will neither abstain from his duty nor perform it flabbily. When he judges, he will take equity as his mentor and guide. "Equity," said Aristotle, "bids us be merciful to the weakness of human nature; to think less about the laws than about the man who framed them, and less about what he said than about what he meant; not to consider the actions of the accused so much as his intentions, nor this or that detail so much as the whole story; to ask not what a man is now but what he has always or usually been. It bids us remember benefits rather than injuries, and benefits received rather than benefits conferred; to be patient when we are wronged; to settle a dispute by negotiation and not by force. . . ."

*The Grading of Belief.* In political affairs, the decisions a man reaches depend mainly on the general principles he happens to believe in and the concrete, particular facts he happens to believe. His beliefs are the working premises for all his activities, ranging from a casual opinion he expresses in a private conversation to a formal vote he casts on election day. As a free man believes so he decides, and as he decides so goes the commonwealth. If our objective is to obtain a higher quality of civic judgment, we must understand how beliefs function and how they should be graded.

Why is it necessary to resort to grading? Because the innumerable beliefs that any of us holds at a given moment are not created equal and cannot be rendered equal in respect of either verification or verifiability. Some have been verified; some have been verified in part; some have not been verified at all; some that have not been verified can be verified; some can be verified slightly, some convincingly, some conclusively; some, in the nature of things, cannot be verified at all. Conclusive verification is usually restricted to phenomena that one can isolate, test, and repeat at will in a laboratory, allowing, of course, for the possibility that the very act of testing may modify even them. Rarely does this apply to political propositions. On entering the realm of the political, even the most rigorous reasoner finds that in most cases he must dispense with laboratory procedures and rely on lesser degrees of verification.

Beginning with Locke and Hume, the great philosophical empiricists have advised us to proportion our respective beliefs to the evidence that supports them. Strict verification is generally impossible. If a belief is about some unique past event, the chances of verifying it will vary enormously. Concerning some incidents of history, we can turn to elaborate and relatively trustworthy records; concerning others we have nothing save the testimony of a single biased author, or of two conflicting authors, or of several authors who lived generations after the event. How, for example, can anyone really verify what Julius Caesar said when he crossed the Rubicon, much less what determined him to cross it? How can anyone verify whether, on Thursday last, a budgetary understanding was reached between the mayor of New York and the governor of the state, an occurrence which one of them now angrily affirms and the other stoutly denies? If a United States senator remained silent, as so many did, during the years of disgraceful McCarthyism (1949—1955), who can verify at a later date whether he intended privately to approve or disapprove the practices of the time? For that matter, how many citizens will take care to ascertain in later times whether the senator did remain silent on the issue of McCarthyism?

If the belief involves a general policy and a prediction of favorable or unfavorable future consequences, we may be able to resort to some limited, preliminary experimentation in order to test it. All social life can be looked at as a congeries of experiments which we have no choice but to make, though many of them furnish us with extremely ambiguous answers. Nor are we prone to accept the answers even when they are clear. We say that every form of government and institution of law is an experiment, yet unless an established form of government becomes insufferable or a familiar legal institution becomes preposterous, most of us will cling to it as it is, insisting the while that the experiment needs only more time, more money, or more devotion—or perhaps a different party in office—to achieve success. After all, since what we predict about future events depends in large part on what we believe about past events and present conditions, the predictions can scarcely be safer or surer than the beliefs that underlie them.

For these reasons, the citizen of quality continually classifies his beliefs as he puts them to use. He reminds himself at every juncture that weak verification and weak verifiability are not equal to strong verification and strong verifiability. When he encounters a problem, he examines his stock of relevant beliefs in order to proportion each of them to the evidence on which it is based. But this is only the beginning of the method. For a second and more decisive step, he proceeds to grade the respective beliefs according to what he conceives the *human cost* that will follow from acting on them. What is clearly a sound belief or a warranted assertion for a low cost in prospective human percussions may not be sound at all if the prospective cost is raised.

Consequently, our citizen of quality feels free to reject the familiar conceptualistic boundary between "belief" and "non-belief." He insists on inserting an intermediate category between them, which he calls "inadequate belief." It is simply not true in human affairs that we either believe and act on our belief or disbelieve and decline to act. A belief may be genuine and sincere, but "inadequate." It is "inadequate" when the persuasive force of the evidence behind it, though quite strong enough for lesser uses, will not support some more momentous and costly course of action that we now have under contemplation.

Let me mention some familiar instances. Suppose on a foggy day you ask whether it is raining, and suppose I have not looked toward the window for some time; I may fairly answer as best I can without further investigation—unless I have reason to consider that you are taking a baby out-of-doors, or are susceptible to pneumonia, or perhaps have wagered heavily on a horse that always loses on a muddy track. If you ask the time of day, I may answer casually and approximately—unless I understood that an error on my part may cause you to miss your plane. Or again, my recollection of the holding in a law case, though firm enough for most purposes, may be inadequate if the case becomes pertinent in preparing a professional opinion, and then I must consult the source. The conceived human cost of acting on a belief is the working criterion of its adequacy.

There are two main centers of cost to begin with: cost to the human *subject* of the conceived action, and cost to the human *object*. The subject inquires what will be the initial cost, what the prospective upkeep and maintenance that the proffered idea may require him to assume, and his belief will be graded according to the highest cost level he feels willing and able to maintain. For example, people may believe quite sincerely in the idea of universal education at one cost level and not believe in it at another. Some may believe sincerely in secular public education, but not at the cost of sending their own children to grossly inferior public schools. Judges may believe sincerely in the idea of speedy justice at the cost level of opening court at ten o'clock, but not at the cost level of nine o'clock.

Then there is the factor of conceived cost to the human object of the action. In this regard, the entire pattern of Anglo-American law endorses the wisdom of grading factual beliefs. If the charge against a man amounts to mere gossip or hearsay, the law refuses to predicate any sort of liability on it. It does not impose liability for money damages unless the arbiter's belief is based on a preponderance of credible evidence; it does not impose civil disabilities for the commission of fraud unless the belief is verified further and is based on clear and convincing proof; and it does not impose a penitentiary sentence for crime unless the belief is entirely firm and is based on proof beyond a reasonable doubt. When the legal system is true to its own best insights, as it is on this score in many democratic states, it acknowledges candidly that the belief of guilt (physical, psychological, and moral) never becomes absolute enough to justify capital punishment. All in all, the practice of considering human impacts as prospective costs not only assists us to grade beliefs critically; it also invites us to distinguish between the initial outlay and the long-term maintenance which a course of action may impose on us and others.

There are two important corollaries to note. For one thing, it follows that when philosophers or scientists urge us to develop new political and ethical standards by using experimental methods, they ought to specify limits for the experiments in terms of human costs. Ever since it was established beyond a reasonable doubt that Nazi German scientists had perpetrated tortures, disfigurements, and wholesale murders while experimenting on human beings, the civilized world has expected the advocates of experimentation to speak forthrightly and explicitly on the subject of limits. If they still say nothing about limits, they are not likely to be heard with respect.

For another thing, since "cost" implies damage or loss or harm to someone, we may fairly accept a much smaller quantum of evidence if all we are asked to credit is something favorable. When the issue involves condemning and punishing, the evidence ought to reach an extremely high level; when it involves filling a major office or determining an important public policy, the evidence ought to be clear and convincing; when it involves filling a minor office or choosing between relatively equal alternatives, the evidence ought to disclose a discernible preponderance for the side that wins favor. But when there is nothing more at stake than a question of granting rewards, bounties, and honorary benefits, we need not be so particular; we can afford to take a risk. In effect, the citizens of a free society are not required to balance the evil and the good in quite the same scales. They can frankly acknowledge a preference for doing whatever seems open-handed and magnanimous.

# VIII

# *Quality: The Virtues of Honor and Associability*

## *An Instance of Honor*

Honor, let us freely affirm at the outset, is an essentially aristocratic quality. It is not comprehended by taking opinion polls or counting ballots; it does not usually belong to the many, and often it becomes most evident when the few repudiate the standards and desires that control the many. But honor's aristocratic nature need not disconcert anyone who understands the ideal purpose of democratic government—which is to produce a society sparkling with the highest possible proportion of authentic patricians.

Whoever seeks the meaning of honor in a democracy has only to contemplate the trial, condemnation, and death of Socrates. Long centuries and millennia ago, in 399 B.C., a certain rather squat personage, some seventy years old, who if left alone would soon have died of natural causes, who had organized no party or institution, had held no public post of importance, had written no books or manifestoes, had, in fact, done little more than wander about his native city asking elementary philosophical questions and, when he received an answer, asking further questions in order to test the answer—this man was indicted, tried, and put to death; and thereupon the world was changed for all time. The drama remains as incandescent as ever. In every generation, men still behold with excitement: How the Athenians, through their insensate arrogance and their foolish passion for Alcibiades, dissipate their alliances, immolate the flower of their youth, and demolish their prosperous empire in the Peloponnesian War; how, yielding to the Spartans, they accept the rule of Critias and the other Thirty Tyrants; how Socrates defies first the democratic majority, in their turn, and then the Thirty Tyrants, in theirs, when they attempt to disregard established laws and commit judicial murders; how after expelling the Thirty the Athenians lust to find a convenient scapegoat for their own blunders and crimes; how they indict Socrates, the noblest and most earnestly religious man among them, on charges of corrupting the youth and undermining the traditional religion; how all Athens knows that although Socrates taught the youthful Alcibiades and Critias, both of them drew far away from him when they became demagogues and tyrants; how Socrates stands straight and steadfast on his trial, declines to cringe to the jury, addresses them with somber dignity, and exalts his philosophic vocation; how he explains simply that, as he was not free to throw down his arms or abandon his post when he stood in the ranks of war, no more can he now disregard God's order to search everlastingly into himself and other men; how he declares that he can never alter his ways, not even if he has to die many times; how, by a majority of thirty votes out of five hundred and one, they hold him guilty; how still refusing to beg for life, he explains that the custom of wailing and groveling is shameful to the accused and discreditable to the judges; how they vote to condemn him to death; and how he tells them at last: "The difficulty, my friends, is not to avoid death but to avoid unrighteousness, for that runs faster than death. I am old and move slowly, and the slower runner has overtaken me, and my accusers are keen and quick, and the faster runner, who is unrighteousness, has overtaken them. . . . The hour of departure has arrived, and we go our ways—I to die, and you to live. Which is better God only knows."

This is the drama that will haunt the imaginations of men as long as there are any that count themselves free. Socrates' closing remark contains no bitterness but the simple truth, for who can say whether to live unfree is really better and more desirable than to die? It depends, one supposes, on the inner image a man has developed to represent his irreducible self. Some people would prefer to continue alive on any terms and at any cost; they would choose any state whatever as an alternative to death; they would repeat, "Better a living dog than a dead lion," without feeling abashed by the thought that even a dog may be willing to give his life for what he considers a higher good. There are human existences that display nothing beyond a statistical value and amount to no more than animated deaths.

But life is not the only sacrifice to consider, nor is dying for one's civic principles the only way to attest them. On the contrary, relatively few principles are worth the cost of life, and these are seldom jeopardized to a critical degree. What indeed would be the advantage of grading our beliefs if a willingness to die for them were the sole and exclusive test of our sincerity? There are various lesser tests that cost much less than death, yet, interestingly enough, these are the ones that seem to disturb men most. Many who will not flinch a moment before the onslaught of war will stand appalled before the threat of a priest's, wife's, employer's, or politician's disapproval. So it was with the Athenians. Brave enough in battling the Spartans, they lacked the rudimentary courage to confront their own blunders and crimes, and therefore they chose to send Socrates to his death. In all probability, they would have been equally willing to condemn anyone and everyone else—including, of course, the Olympian gods, if these had not already grown weary of bearing the blame for human follies and taken to diverting themselves with more promising experiments. The truth of the matter is that citizens can never be fit company for their fellows, much less for the gods, until they learn to live with their own deeds; nor can a Socrates be safe in any time or country until the people put all possible scapegoats out to pasture.

How, then, would Socrates fare today among us? R. H. S. Crossman, a prominent English intellectual and Member of Parliament, has the following to say:

> To appreciate, therefore, the tragedy of Socrates' execution, we must realize that it was politically justifiable. The statesman must consider the results of a policy or a creed, and not merely the motives behind it. Looked at from this point of view, Socrates' guilt was proved up to the hilt. His teaching had inspired the counterrevolution, and his theology had produced, not a puritan revival, but a ruthless and cynical gang of wealthy adventurers. The fact that he had denounced their philosophy of force did not make any material difference. His disciples had welcomed his attacks on current morality, and disregarded the positive side of his creed.
>
> The responsibilities of the teacher are great. He must consider not only whether his teachings are true, but what effect they will have on his pupils. In the eyes of the practical politician it is no justification of Socrates as a teacher to show that he denounced wickedness, if his virtuous teachings, in fact, promoted it. However blameless his life and pure his motives, the effects on Athenian life had been disastrous. When we remember this, we cannot blame the jury which found him guilty of corrupting the youth.

If Mr. Crossman is right, then Socrates must have been either a great knave or an egregious fool, and possibly more than a little of each. On the one hand, it would have been knavish of him to continue with teachings that had been proved so "disastrous" to the commonwealth and, on the other hand, it would have been foolish to announce at his trial that he would never change or desist. One would suppose that if he was indeed a fool his talks and dialogues could scarcely have caused such extensive harm, and if he was indeed a knave he would probably have answered his accusers more discreetly. If Mr. Crossman is right, then Plato must have been mocking when he called Socrates "the wisest and justest and best of all men of his time," and modern libertarians like Thomas Jefferson and John Adams must have been jesting when they ranked Socrates beside Jesus of Nazareth. According to Mr. Crossman's singular notion of "the responsibilities of a teacher," it is not safe even to teach the truth, to lead a blameless life, and to obey the purest of motives because if some of one's pupils should disregard "the positive side" of one's creed and become "a ruthless and cynical gang," one's guilt is "proved up to the hilt." Should the notion be accepted generally, the profession of teaching would become a most hazardous occupation, for who could ever foretell how a vicious pupil—or for that matter a vicious reader in a later epoch—might misuse and misapply one's precepts?

One cannot but stand in awe before Mr. Crossman's conception of the power a teacher exerts over human deeds and destinies. He believes, and asks us to believe, that whatever Alcibiades did was the "effect" of Socrates' teachings. (Oddly enough, he gives no affirmative credit for various other pupils of Socrates who became virtuous and faithful supporters of the Athenian democracy.) On similar reasoning, one would infer that the Spanish Inquisition was the "effect" of Jesus' teachings. We are expected to forget everything we know about the mind, temperament, and nurture of Alcibiades, the indulgence he received from Pericles, his guardian, the passionate imbecility of the Athenian populace in following him when he was wrong and attacking him when he was right, and every other motive, cause, and factor in his vertiginous career—save only the youthful conversations with Socrates. What a strange concept of psychological causation this is, and what a curious standard by which to decide whether a pedagogue ought to die! Fortunately for education and educators in England and elsewhere, most men do not think as Mr. Crossman does; they do not regard a teacher as a sort of official puppeteer or toymaker, who deserves to be punished, no matter how worthy his efforts, if any of his puppets should subsequently misbehave or go astray.

Puppets and puppeteers are scarcely the analogues for education and judgment in a free society. What Mr. Crossman's position would require of us is tantamount to what the Athenian prosecutors required of Socrates, which he could by no means bring himself to yield—a threefold surrender of human dignity. This was the trial's ultimate stake. First, there was Socrates' own dignity as teacher, philosopher, religious believer, patriot, and human being. Second, there was the dignity of his *polis*, the community and country that, if true to itself, might edify Greece and the world, as he had sought to edify it. How could he submit to repression and censorship without degrading Athens, or grovel to the court without shaming the processes of Athenian justice?

Finally, and in addition to these, there was a third dignity at stake. Though contemned by the Athenian populace, it too has a proper claim on our consideration and respect. It is the dignity that belonged to Alcibiades and Critias, both of whose lives had come to an end years before the trial of Socrates. They too were rational beings, responsible in politics, ethics, and the annals of history for their own decisions and actions, entitled to reward for their public services and deserving of punishment for their wrongs. They were no puppets but men—strong, intelligent, willful men, at that. Their careers, accomplishments, and defects were their own; they belonged no more to Socrates than, two generations later, the vast conquests achieved by Alexander the Great would belong to his tutor, Aristotle.

Paying tribute to this threefold human dignity, Socrates calmly accepted the sentence of death. His example is an enduring and trustworthy beacon for free men everywhere. Fortunately, as matters go under normal conditions, the citizens of a democratic polity do not have to wager anything so costly as their lives in order to keep their liberties intact. Much smaller sacrifices and cheaper resistances will usually deter officials from attempts at encroachment. But let us be candid with one another: there is never a time when the willingness to die can be dispensed with or cast in doubt. Land by land, freedom glows and flames or flickers out according to that willingness.

### *Associability*

Associability, which adds the strictly democratic note to the chord of good citizenship, is the quality that fits one to cooperate as an equal in the work of a group or institution. An associable person gives the group its full due by contributing a store of information for its use, submitting his opinions for general consideration, respectfully weighing those of other members, deliberating before he takes a final position, accepting the group's decision with good grace, and doing his functional share to put it into effect. Associability holds equal men together when they disagree. It prompts the members of a minority party to support laws and measures that the majority may have thrust on them against their interests and inclinations, and it prompts the majority to exercise reasonableness, moderation, and restraint because some day they too may suffer the vicissitudes of political fortune and come to occupy the place of a minority. To be associable one must feel respect for his fellow citizens.

But not too much. Associability in any proper sense implies neither conformism nor servile demolatry. It does not sweeten a cup of hemlock. The better kind of associable citizen will exert his own critical faculties and never confuse the majority's right to have its way with the majority's being right in the specific way it chooses. He will not allow a popular vote to stultify his mind or overwhelm his conscience. Since, moreover, the quality of associability has little to do with being merely gregarious or consorting indiscriminately with others, a person who considers the majority ignorant, gullible, shallow, alien, and crass, can nevertheless conduct himself associably if he honors the boundary between his own civic functions and theirs.

A citizen takes his first rational step toward associability when he becomes aware that in his polity certain civic functions are assigned to him while certain others are not. He cannot perform his functions satisfactorily if, like the obsessive busybodies who infested Athenian society and whom Aristophanes caricatured in *The Wasps,* he neglects his family and business, meddles in public activities that he does not understand, and endeavors to direct the entire apparatus of government. A citizen is worth little to the state who does not know how to go his quiet, private way and enjoy his home in peace. Unless he prizes a private sector of existence for himself, he will never appreciate its worth for others or yield them a respite. In short, like most other virtues and skills, associability may range far afield but it ought to begin at home.

We have discussed the people's functions in a democratic society and their right to make basic political decisions. In supporting this right, we offered no roseate view of human nature, no promise of its perfectibility, no easy guarantee that, though many people act like morons or brutes today, they will all act like wise and gentle souls tomorrow. Perhaps more of them will, perhaps there are some indications of social advance, perhaps the bigots with their thin lips and flinty hearts are really dwindling in number and power, and perhaps the gradual progress of liberty and equality on the world scene can cast a veil over recent events that added the word "genocide" to civilization's vocabulary. At any rate, when we speak on behalf of the popular majority and their rights, let us confront the facts realistically. There are many so-called democracies—old ones as well as new—where the masses of the people are illiterate, uninformed, and woefully unprepared for the responsibilities of self-rule. Even in countries like the United States and Great Britain, the various forms of censorship, arising as they do out of emotional insecurity, neurotic fear, and the impulse to accept authoritarian domination, are not alien to the common people but congenial to very many of them. When we declare the democratic maxim that the masses of the people possess good intentions, freedom of choice, and a modicum of rationality, all we can fairly affirm is a net advantage for honesty and a long-term, deep-seated propensity for justice. These are our maximum claims.

Yet they are clearly enough to establish the working value of democracy, at least as long as the channels of information and communication stay open for public use and discussion. As Aristotle discerned, there is much more worth and wisdom to the people's judgment than one can possibly discover by merely examining the single judgments of isolated individuals and adding them in columnar tabulations. Separately, the citizens may seem ignorant and callous beyond the limits of tolerance. But bring them together as an electorate, assemble them in a hall, congregate them via the newspapers, convert the individuals into a community, and you cumulate their experience, pool their information, and refine their sensibility. Once they come together, unless they are debased and vicious in character, the people are the only dependable judges—at least of those things that they can personally consume or use. In a consumer perspective, it is they and not the experts who must pass the eventual judgment. Aristotle would rather have the tenant than the expert builder judge the house. If we conceive of public discussion as a kind of meal or banquet, then it is easy to understand that each ordinary citizen brings along his own experience and contributes in his way to an aggregate that often excels anything a philosopher could contrive. Though some of the philosopher's concoctions may be more elegant, the general mass of citizens are the ones who finally consume the political fare and thrive or suffer by it. Hence Aristotle remarked shrewdly, "The diner—not the cook—will be the best judge of a feast."

A memorable aphorism, and one that an intelligent citizen can accept without believing either that the political feast is particularly nutritious and succulent in his time or that the majority's taste is impeccable. He can accept the aphorism and nevertheless persist in trying to improve both the feast and the general taste. He can accept it when the question belongs to public policy while rejecting it when the question belongs to private conscience, theology, or theoretical science. If he chooses, he can accept the aphorism not as a commendation of the dining public, but merely as an admonition and chastening reminder to the officials in the political kitchen. And if he accepts it in any of these applications, employs it to inform his political appraisals, and resists every attempt to abridge the public's right of discussion and judgment, he exemplifies the true value of associability.

Insofar as associability requires a citizen to collaborate with the standards and predilections of the majority, it does induce a certain recurrent tension in him between impulsions toward conformity and impulsions toward independent self-expression. In this respect,

De Tocqueville's observations were correct. The man of quality is *not* identical with the man of equality. Far from coinciding effortlessly within an intelligent and sensitive psyche, the two of them frequently clash and collide. They meet like Jacob and the strange man in the Bible story, who come together on a deserted riverbank at evening, wrestle with each other all through the darkness of the night, and still cling, each to the other, when the sun rises in the morning (Genesis 32:23-30). If we take Jacob, the concrete striving individual, as exemplifying a man of quality, then we may also take his nameless and mysterious adversary, who seems more like an abstract symbol than a living person, as exemplifying the man of equality. According to the Bible legend, the anonymous wrestler touches Jacob in the thigh and wounds him so that he will limp slightly for the remainder of his life, and perhaps this too offers an allegory for the fate befalling certain men of quality in democratic societies. Nevertheless, though wounded, Jacob still clutches the awesome visitor tightly and refuses to let go until he exacts a blessing from him.

More than a century after De Tocqueville, the tension continues between the two forces, unresolved and unrelieved. In dire accents, the American intellectuals of every succeeding generation denounce the manifestations of conformism that characterize their own era and despondently predict the approach of cultural darkness. They are invariably correct, though sometimes rather hyperbolic, in their descriptions, and—thus far, at least—mistaken in their prophecies. Each new generation seems to supply not only a plethora of conformists but also a fair quota of independent, gifted, and curiously distinctive figures in the various dynamic areas of the culture. Meanwhile, apocalyptic visions continue of an America of total sameness and dispirited homogeneity.

If De Tocqueville had lived a century later than he did, he would have enjoyed meeting and observing Louis D. Brandeis, who served on the United States Supreme Court from 1916 to 1939 and demonstrated quite clearly that a democratic citizen can retain his individuality and independence while reaching the heights of civic associability. Merely seeing Brandeis was an experience. He had a tall, angular, wiry figure, which became slightly stooped as the years passed, and a beautifully formed head with hair that was always recalcitrant and unruly; in the last part of his life he allowed it to grow and wander as it would. No one who saw those deeply set blue-gray eyes of his would ever forget how quick and brilliant they were. Perhaps his mouth was his most revealing feature, because even in old age the lips still remained sensitive and full as though to show his vitality and zestfulness—and yet at the corners the mouth would purse a bit, as though to admonish that reason and self-discipline were the constant masters of his spirit. If you knew him at all, you were not surprised that nature had given him a strong chin, in fact, you might wonder why it did not project farther. A dedicated champion of civil liberty and industrial democracy, Brandeis had a sense of injustice reminiscent of the ancient Hebrew prophets. President Franklin D. Roosevelt habitually referred to him as "Isaiah."

Before his appointment to the Supreme Court, Brandeis had made himself famous as an opponent of the great trusts and monopolies; he had waged a relentless campaign against entrenched economic power and massive concentrations of wealth. In the industrial world, he believed that bigness was a curse, not only because the giant corporation might crush the small businessman, not only because it might depersonalize human relationships, but specifically because bigness was often clumsy, unmanageable, wasteful, dropsical, and therefore stupid. Continually he worked to build a society where a man would be able to find room and move around, a society athrob with novelty and creative invention, where at any given moment countless experiments might be under way to discover better and still better methods to produce and distribute merchandise and—what was more important—to adjust and harmonize human relations. In a world where change had become rapid and drastic, Brandeis believed that only the land of the alert, the daring and the experimental would be found fit to survive. Such was the lifelong vision of this methodical, incisive, and painstaking lawyer, who could derive as much delight from economic statistics and sociological data as from revised statutes and legal precedents. Whatever his other qualities and excellences, would one take him as a likely model of associability?

It was some years after Brandeis' death before the issuance of a volume of his *unpublished* opinions revealed the extent of his associability on the bench. Possibly only lawyers and judges can realize what the suppressing of these documents—no mere drafts but complete and polished products of endless searchings, composings, and revisings—must have cost Brandeis. Curious as it may seem to laymen, every lawyer knows that every other lawyer (save only himself) pants and rages with a virulent pride of authorship. In Brandeis' instance, how much proper occasion there was for pride! A perfectionist as judicial craftsman, he tirelessly rewrote his opinions in version after version, dozens and scores of times, in one instance fifty-three times, in an effort to make them just a bit more lucid, more coherent, and more instructive.

Behind each of his resolves to withhold an opinion from publication there was a subtle and complex drama in the repertory of associability. He had suppressed this one because the mere reading of it had persuaded a colleague to change his vote on the case, that one because a colleague had responded by inserting a suitable phrase in his own draft to embody Brandeis' reasoning, this one because the time and case did not seem quite ripe to press a new theory of law, and that one because he had decided to subordinate his warranted pride to institutional prestige and the maintenance of harmony. In the long history of the Court, no justice was ever more concerned for its dignity and integrity as an institution. We may say that he made its integrity his own. There is a time to display one's work and a time to seclude it, and he who chooses the right time can satisfy his pride as well one way as the other.

Nevertheless, all this line of behavior, meritorious though it really was, operated only within the chambers of the Court. It was admirable enough but its scene was restricted. For a more public example, we can turn to one of his famous dissenting opinions which demonstrated the quality of associability on a heroic scale.

It seems that in 1925 the State of Oklahoma enacted that, the manufacture of ice for sale being a public business, no one must engage in it in any Oklahoma community without obtaining a license from a state commission. The commission was not to grant a license to any new applicant whenever it found, after investigation and a hearing, that the local community already had sufficient facilities for the manufacture and sale of ice. In effect, the ice company that was already established in any community would enjoy a monopoly as long as its services and facilities were considered adequate; it would be protected by state law against the emergence of competitors. If ever a statute flouted Brandeis' economic convictions, this one did.

A few years later, the United States Supreme Court (6 to 2) declared the Oklahoma statute unconstitutional. Under our Constitution, the Court held, the state could grant a monopoly status to a railroad or public utility but could not prevent any person from entering an ordinary business. Since the manufacture of ice was an ordinary business, the state could only regulate it in the public interest; it could not preclude anyone from engaging in it or establish a network of local monopolies.

With this outcome a smaller person than Brandeis would have been quite satisfied, for it enforced his own economic tenets of pluralism and free competition and gave them constitutional sanction. Yet in ringing terms Brandeis dissented. For one thing, the calendar told him that the year was 1932, the darkest and most despairing declivity of the Great Depression. For another, he called to mind the bounds and limits of the Court's function in passing on the constitutionality of social and economic legislation. How could the Court assume to weigh the practical desirability of the Oklahoma law and nullify it as unnecessary and undesirable? "Our function," he protested, "is only to determine the reasonableness of the legislature's belief in the existence of evils and in the effectiveness of the remedy provided." Five years later, after the historic crisis between President Roosevelt and the Court, the majority of the justices finally returned to this modest and reasonable view of their function, and today it stands as one of our system's enduring cornerstones.

Brandeis felt no scintilla of confidence in what the Oklahoma legislature was attempting to accomplish. To him the experiment seemed futile, unwise, even injurious. Yet he comprehended not only the nature of his own function and its disparity to the legislature's; he also comprehended the economic plight of the American people. He would not close his eyes to what all men knew, or read the law in books only and not in streets, factories, and homes. Defending therefore the constitutionality of a statute that he regarded as regressive and obnoxious, Brandeis wrote:

> The people of the United States are now confronted with an emergency more serious than war. Misery is widespread in a time, not of scarcity, but of over-abundance. The long-continued depression has brought unprecedented unemployment, a catastrophic fall in commodity prices and a volume of economic losses which threatens our financial institutions.
>
> . . . . There must be power in the States and the Nation to remould, through experimentation, our economic practices and institutions to meet changing social and economic needs.
>
> . . . . This Court has the power to prevent an experiment. We may strike down the statute which embodies it on the ground, that in our opinion, the measure is arbitrary, capricious or unreasonable . . . But in the exercise of this high power, we must be ever on guard, lest we erect our prejudices into legal principles. If we would guide by the light of reason, we must let our minds be bold.

### *Quality and the Democratic Community*

We have summarized the main capacities and powers of a democratic man of quality, the "virtues and talents" that equip him to exercise critical and compassionate judgment, maintain his civic honor, and collaborate intelligently in group undertakings. Each of these powers requires frequent practice, and tends to atrophy unless it is put to active use. Like an athlete, the man of quality must not only flex his civic muscles from time to time; he must also maintain, somewhere in the regimen of his life, a special area for the rehearsing of discipline, austerity, and self-denial.

For example, in the early days of ancient Rome, Manius Curius Dentatus, consul of the republic, lived in a meager cottage, and when the ambassadors of the Samnites came to offer him a bribe on behalf of their nation, they found him cooking some turnips for his meal. Dentatus' answer was ready: "A man who can be satisfied with such a supper has no need of gold." Socrates, in his way, kept his life immune from the material lusts and dependences that weaken a mind to temptation. He would pause and stare at the rows of luxurious merchandise in the fairs of imperial Athens, then say to himself, "How many things I can do without!" Brandeis too, though wealthy, practiced an almost ascetic austerity. Under the conditions of modern democratic life, it is scarcely necessary to do without palatable food or gay ornaments. Nowadays, the most seductive variety of merchandise, which a man of quality must always stand prepared to renounce, is something rather less tangible; it is the approval of the populace.

Yet a man of personal integrity and intellectual independence does not need to look with disdain on the general community, its standards, or its judgments. On the contrary, he ought to acknowledge that he can only offer back to the community what he has already learned and taken from it. True, with his distinctive virtues, labors, talents, and in exceptional cases his unique genius, he may have reshaped, colored, and animated the practices and aspirations that he found about him. But it is the community that invariably provides the cultural substance and the political matrix. What he conceives to be his own thesis is merely a response on his part to environmental stimuli. The community teaches him what in turn it needs to learn from him and what gestures he must make to gain its attention and communicate with it. It not only poses the meaningful questions; it also proffers the raw materials and specifications for the answers. Socrates' answers, though the Athenian majority may have disliked them, were typically Athenian and could scarcely have been developed, tested, or disseminated in any other ancient society. Brandeis' thought was characteristically American. In politics as elsewhere, nothing can be gathered unless the seasons, the seed, and the soil consent, and though through care and skill a crop of figs may be increased, they will never take root in the desert sand or grow from thistles.

Under ordinary circumstances, a citizen of quality will find himself sharing the opinions of a large, if not a major, segment of his community, and this general concurrence, extending as it does to the chief maxims and patterns of political life, makes it easier for him to acquiesce and cooperate when he happens to enter an area of disagreement. He understands that public judgments are frequently wiser in their practical conclusions than in the theoretical arguments given to explain them. As he looks back on the long train of his own political judgments and acknowledges inwardly how many of them have proved erroneous, he may come to acquire a reasonable modesty. In any case, he does not expect to escape the recurrent burden of investigating sources, assembling evidence, and estimating future consequences and human costs. He understands that if public judgments are usually sound enough for him, it is because certain other members of the public have felt these duties and taken these pains.

Nevertheless, even as a community is always considerably more than a polity, so a man is always considerably more than a citizen. If man is a political animal, he is certainly also an apolitical one. He leads both kinds of existence daily during the same life span. We can never be comprehended wholly in our citizenship or committed entirely to any political allegiance. Divide us through as often as you will and by what institutional divisors you choose; we never come out quite finished and even. Invariably we display some stubborn residue, some recalcitrant and intractable remainder. That is why government would always be a shoddy thing without art, an ignorant thing without science, a dull thing without jollity and play, a stupid and shallow thing without philosophy and religion. Without these, there would be no citizen of quality. A good state requires them as much as all the powers, departments, and offices of government; they are necessary to its mere existence and indispensable to its lasting worth.

In final analysis, the state that attempts to politicalize the inner spontaneities and seclusions of its people only impoverishes them and itself. Private hours are what we shall never be able to do without. It is all very well for the stern sentry whom we call "civic obligation" to keep asking, "Who goes there? Who goes there?" A person needs plenty of time and privacy to make certain of the answer before he can give it.

# IX

# *The Representation of Free Men*

## *The Intolerable, the Tolerable, and the Uniquely Desirable*

Having come this far, we may pause long enough to look back at the road and take our bearings. At the outset we saw that the chief difficulty with democratic man's new moral position was its perplexing vagueness, which exposed him just as much to false anxieties and fancied guilts as to deserved and genuine ones. Lost in obscurity, his imagination was left to wander at large and conjure a hideous train of complicities. The very government which he had set up to embody his ideals and perform his purposes appeared to have become a core of continual moral infection. His predicament was worse than politically dangerous; it was ethically and psychologically intolerable.

Confronting this state of affairs, we resolved that we should never be able to cope with it unless we first dispelled the enveloping miasma of vagueness. If vagueness was what induced the anxiety and carried the moral contagion, then the only practical remedy must consist in attaining precision and specification; these must be our immediate objectives. The sequel proved how useful they were, for no sooner had we divided the subject matter according to the most fundamental of distinctions—the distinction between collective responsibility and individual responsibility—than the whole irksome predicament began to appear manageable and tolerable.

Our analysis went on to show that the duties of collective responsibility were not so heavy as to exceed the economic and ethical potential of a self-respecting democratic community; they required only a more conscious exertion of intelligence, foresight, and civic solidarity. When, in turn, we addressed ourselves to the duties of individual responsibility, we found these too were readily susceptible to limitation and definition—by means of the citizen's Self-Search. The Self-Search conferred precision and clarity on the entire condition. It apportioned the burden of accessory guilt according to the individual's own doings, lapses, and deserts. It offered him a defined and rational way to exonerate himself from moral complicity if he really merited exoneration. By establishing specific categories and precise criteria, our analysis served to trim the onus of responsibility to tolerable dimensions and adjust it fairly on the shoulders of the individual citizen.

Then we turned to a happier topic—to the vital incentives, the social faculties, and the personal fulfillments that characterize democratic existence, straighten the shoulders of the citizen, and infuse them with necessary strength. The life of man in an open society is not confined to assuming solemn duties, bearing heavy responsibilities, and dragging moral burdens. While the responsibilities of our condition are genuine, so too are the incentives and the attainable rewards. The citizens of free countries need not remain satisfied—as others must—with a political condition that is only tolerable. They are entitled to a mode of life that is abundant and ardently desirable. Passive equality sets a floor under their deprivations and misfortunes while active equality removes the ceiling from their opportunities and incites them to the adventures of self-fulfillment. Yet civic quality excels even these gratifications and proffers the supreme incentives of democratic life: intelligence and compassion in the exercise of judgment, courage and integrity in the exercise of honor, and self-disciplined allegiance in the exercise of associability.

If a citizen has profited from these exercises, he will frankly recognize the vagaries in human behavior and the weaknesses in popular government and will abstain from judging either the electorate or the officials by utopian or perfectionist standards. Though his mood may vary according to the season, even in his most cynical hours he will refuse to imagine himself as living willingly under a totalitarian regime. How do people endure from day to day, he wonders, when they are not able to think what they choose, speak what they think, and laugh as they will at the officials? He shakes his head in pity. What a truncated kind of existence! Whoever cannot summon those who rule over him to the court of conscience seems somehow less than a man. Of this he feels absolutely certain: Whatever else representative democracy may imply in human relations, it must imply that everything of moral import in the transactions of government is perpetually subject to moral examination, criticism, and judgment.

### *The Justice of Administration*

Service in a government continually subject to moral judgment calls for capacities that authoritarian regimes may consider irrelevant or even inimical. Under a democratic system, competence and skill are not enough to deserve public office, nor are personal magnetism and the aura of military victories. In point of fact, no combination of talents can ever suffice unless a firm moral character controls them. Fortunately, there are many public officers in the free nations who display this indispensable qualification, reflecting credit on themselves and their constituents and proving that the democratic moral standard is neither unrealistic nor utopian but reasonable and practicable. Theirs is the standard of the Just Official.

Under a representative system the Just Official may be found serving any of a variety of functions. He may be president, senator, or sheriff, judge, city councilman, or sergeant of police. Whatever the duties in his assigned function, we do not consider him a Just

Official unless he is alert and vigorous in performing them. If plans are his duty to devise, the Just Official prepares them; if public consent and support are his to obtain, he works to earn them; and if judgment and discretion are his to employ, he accepts the responsibility and puts them to work. He is not too bemused to lead or decide. Though quite aware that his accomplishments are subject to human faults and frailties, he does not temper the earnestness of his effort.

Nevertheless, before embarking on any program that has conceivable moral import—whether it affects many, a few, or only one—he excuses himself to external interlocutors, shuts out the loud clamors of interest and the seductive whispers of habituation, and privately scrutinizes the findings of his conscience. The questions he confronts will include the following, at very least:

## The Democratic Official's Self-Search

**I.** How would the contemplated action appear to the public if *all* the facts, interests, motives, and profits were divulged?

**II.** How would it appear if the consequences (by which you propose to justify it) should be entirely different from those you expect?

**III.** If, uneasy about a proposed act, you find yourself arguing that it is a familiar practice in which almost everyone indulges, then test your position by assuming that yours is the sole instance and you *alone* have committed such an act; what do you think of it in this light?

**IV.** If a tempting misdeed promises to keep or advance you in office and thus enable you to do much future good, is not the evil of the act certain, the good of the promise contingent, and the whole excuse a self-deception?

**V.** If you had never been in public office, how would the contemplated act appear to you as an ordinary member of the community whose authority made it possible?

**VI.** How would you characterize the act if it had been done by your most detested political adversary?

**VII.** In view of these considerations, do you believe that the act would cast honor on the community or would put it to shame?

The Self-Search, as we see, is a preparation and rehearsal for a thoroughgoing public search. Whatever his party connections and allegiances, the Just Official feels a special obligation of candor to the entire democratic electorate. Far from resenting comments and inquiries, he believes that the people are entitled to complete disclosure of public affairs, and that officials who withhold information are generally protecting partisan interests or private political, industrial, and military reputations rather than the legitimate confidences of government. On the other hand, he scarcely expects that the people, once they receive the information, will reduce it to a series of systematic formulas, scientific paradigms, and scholars' syllogisms. Political life—insofar as it is life—declines to become domesticated or tidy, and popular electorates seem to sense that syllogisms are more convenient in defending decisions than in reaching them. The democratic elector utilizes information according to his own experiences and his own modes of feeling and thought. While these are palpably deficient in science and logic, they are generally enlightened enough to avert the kind of ridiculous excesses and inhuman extremes that theoreticians, with relentless consistency, sanctioned during the French Revolution and again during the German Nazi regime. Drunk on reason today, drunk on unreason tomorrow.

The people's right to obtain information does not, of course, depend on any assured ability to understand its significance or use it wisely. Facts belong to the people simply because they relate to interests that are theirs, government that is theirs, and votes that they may desire to cast, for they are entitled to an active role in shaping every fundamental decision of state. "Just think," said John Dewey in a fervent affirmation, "just think what a difference it makes whether you begin with the people and end with the politicians, or begin with the politicians and end by putting something over on the people."

There is an obverse side to the matter of truth, for if the government ought not lie to the people, neither ought the people lie to the government. Democracy's foundations are weakened whenever members of the public do not feel safe in dealing veraciously with their judges, representatives, and officers. This grave peril our Just Official endeavors systematically to avert as far as his functions permit. He scans his country's laws and regulations to ascertain whether they are likely to induce, or even compel, citizens to lie to the government, and discovers that some of them need immediate correction. For example, in a certain country (not the United States) he notes a law providing that packages to be mailed abroad shall be exempt from export duty if their market value is less than, say, $10 but subject to a duty of 50 per cent of the entire value if it exceeds $10; clearly, with precipitous, ungraduated rates like these, the law makes lying profitable enough and detection improbable enough to criminalize large portions of the citizenry. For like reasons, he disapproves: a levy based on the value of the citizens' home furnishings and personal effects which they are required to declare annually under oath; an excise imposed on articles manufactured by workers in the privacy of their homes; and a law requiring anyone accused of crime to testify under oath against himself. Our Just Official strives valiantly to have all such laws reformed or repealed.

He is also watchful of the people's moods, which sometimes require cooling and subduing on the part of the government if they are not to flare out in savage excitements. He recognizes in his own human constitution—why need he feel ashamed of it, disparage it, or deny it?—a constant nonrational heat which, when blended with sense and intelligence, provides the indispensable impulsion for all that is good, beautiful, vital, and compassionate in his experience but which, when intensified beyond control and released in wild outbursts, devastates everything valuable in the vicinity. Our Just Official rightly assumes that his neighbors' constitutions are essentially similar to his, that they too need to keep their nonrational forces channeled for useful service. As reason without emotion becomes psychotic in social relationships, emotion without reason eventually becomes feral. Consequently, the Just Official does not sit at ease in his club, consume a lavish meal, and then condemn the irrationalities of the hungry; nor does he wonder why ignorant men seem so fearful and unemployed men so hate-ridden. Esteeming the people too much to incite the sleeping tiger in them, he does his utmost to prevent group deprivations and remove social grievances.

Regarding his own functions in the government, he freely grants that, whatever safeguards he and his official subordinates may adopt, the possibility of harmful errors simply cannot be eliminated. Perhaps it is some careless lapse that will inflict the damage, or some trivial misunderstanding, some failure of mechanism, or some unforeseeable accident; one way or another, government operations necessarily cause a certain number of losses, mistakes, injustices, and injuries. Acknowledging this unhappy risk as candor requires, the Just Official resolves on a threefold agenda of responsibility. If injuries necessarily result from the transactions and workings of his department, then, for one thing, he never ceases searching for more effective means of prevention. For another, he insists on keeping the channels of public protest open and active. And since in the instances where a harm has already befallen it is too late for prevention and protest to discharge the collective responsibility, our Just Official addresses the legislature assiduously to advocate the passage of general laws for payment of reparation. (He does not quite understand how his official colleagues who have been silent on the subject can rest at night.)

As for him, he thinks well of the people and their instincts, their concern for others at home and abroad, their attachment to liberty, their generosity and sudden good sense, and their fundamental love of peace. Because he does not understand his own motives and impulses totally, he does not require to understand theirs totally. Their tastes and his seem often to disagree, their culture seems shallow, their ideas somewhat confused, and their memories short; nevertheless he is never moved to infer that he is categorically right in his choices and they are wrong. He has a relaxed way of quoting John Locke's remark, "Men may choose different things, yet all choose right." And occasionally when some dogmatic zealot comes to demand that the government invade the people's privacy, censor their amusements, and make them right-minded whether they like it or not, he listens with quiet patience and sits back reflecting; then he smiles gently to his visitor, leans forward again, and answers along the following lines:

"Many years ago there were three foxes who, while crossing a river together, were swept into a hole in the rocks and could not get out. For a long time as they lay there, they suffered miserably from swarms of fleas that fastened on them. A friendly hedgehog came along and offered to brush off the fleas. 'No, thank you,' replied the first fox. 'By this time, these fleas are full and are not sucking much blood. If you remove them, others with fresh appetites will come along and drink all the blood I have left.' The second fox gave a different answer. 'Thank you, Hedgehog,' he said. 'Please go right ahead. I am suffering too much to keep these fleas a moment longer. I'll take my chance on new ones that may come along.' And the third fox stayed silent for a long while, thinking and deliberating. Finally, he spoke: 'Mr. Hedgehog, you are very kind. Both of my brothers are right and both of them are wrong. As for me, I prefer you remove only the fleas on my back where I cannot reach to scratch them. The rest I will either remove myself or learn somehow to live with.' Shortly after, when the foxes succeeded in freeing themselves, the third fox was acclaimed as the sage of all their tribe, and his casual sayings are quoted as proverbs of wisdom to this day."

### *The Democratic Resolution*

In ancient times, the prophets of religion described a vision of such brilliance, beauty, and intensity that it has dazzled men's imaginations ever since. They pictured a sort of Golden Age—not, as the pagans said, hidden in the mists of the remote past but somewhere predictably ahead in the prospects of the future—when men would cease waging war against one another, would live in peace and quiet each under his own vine and fig tree, and would need no external regulation because their own hearts and inward parts would direct them rightly. When that day came, there would be no further occasion for governments, officials, punishments, or laws; men would be free to follow their own benevolent impulses.

The vision arose, of course, because of what the prophets and sages saw when they looked at governments and laws in their time: the apparently irresistible power of despots in Assyria, Babylonia, and Egypt, and subsequently in Macedon and Rome; the brutal systems of compulsion calling themselves governments; the codified injustices passing for laws; the scoundrels and hypocrites sitting as judges; and the desperate condition of the oppressed economic classes. If one could never expect that government would learn the ways of justice, one was driven to hope that justice would abolish government. Laws becoming more inflexible and judges more callous day by day, it seemed that God and man must turn from them and order the world in a radically different way, for even if, incredibly enough, some government or other should begin to act fairly and justly, it would nevertheless employ the old, repulsive methods of power and show the same ugly blotches of force and bloodshed. When the millennial age arrived to replace violence and oppression with harmony and freedom, all laws and governments would simply disappear.

The vision has flourished in almost every era since it was first announced, offering solace to a variety of religious mystics and quietists, encouragement to cooperative experiments such as Brook Farm, and occasional inflammation to the enterprises of anarchists. It attained a sensational though fugitive prominence in Marxist doctrine when Engels, in the name of dialectical materialism, said that the political state was only a transitional institution, and predicted that after the communist revolution it would "wither away," Lenin followed with certain ambiguous statements that seemed to support the notion, and lesser Soviet theoreticians committed the indiscretion—for which they paid heavily in the purges of the 1930's—of treating the "withering away" as something that might come about soon and in Russia. Whether in a religious or a secular formulation, the vision still remains able to fascinate some highly diverse minds; to a world weary of oppression and conflict it apparently offers an ideal image of freedom and peace.

Nevertheless, like other utopian conceptions, it has also done some practical harm. People who trust that an approaching millennium will eradicate all social evils may be less concerned to resist them in the meanwhile, and people who believe that their institutions are so irredeemable that they must ultimately disappear or "wither away" may be slow to reform them. The millennial vision, while it offers men a noble social ideal, likewise provides them with a plausible excuse for accepting the *status quo* and leading a selfish, apolitical existence. Who would take the risks involved in struggling for justice and reform if all law were by nature brutal and all government by necessity oppressive? Until the millennium arrived and brought a society of perfect cooperation, one might do worse than attend to his own interest, pursue his own advantage, and try at whatever cost to survive. Law and government, one could argue, were merely necessary evils ordained to men by reason of their congenital sinfulness. Anyone bent on leading a virtuous life had better keep as far from them as possible.

Thus the ancient prophetic vision, for all its loftiness, exhibited deeply ambivalent implications. It extolled freedom and simultaneously put it beyond practical reach, compassionated the oppressed and impliedly deferred their liberation, criticized the evils of law and seemed to immunize them from correction. By picturing the time when the wolf would dwell beside the lamb, it let men infer that they need not improve the breed of their sheepdogs. These contradictions presented a profound dilemma.

The democratic resolution of the dilemma is, I believe, mankind's greatest single achievement in the ordering of political relations—an accomplishment of such wisdom, judgment, and insight that we are warranted in calling it corporate genius. To state it summarily first before mentioning its implications, the resolution consists, as it were, in *discounting the millennium* by realizing its promise of complete freedom here and now and by compressing it into the realms of conscience, thought, belief, and opinion. This resolution requires endless perseverance for a community to maintain, for no experiments are so difficult as those that grasp a slice of utopia and convert it into present reality. It is here and now, according to the democratic resolution, that a man possesses his full freedom of thought, the vine of his belief, and the fig tree of his conscience; in enjoying them he is completely secure, and government exists to serve as his safeguard. No creed, dogma, or orthodoxy can be imposed to constrict the free play of his intelligence.

For obvious reasons, the democratic formula does not provide a similar immunity to anyone's overt, social behavior; actions that may affect the welfare and safety of others must, of course, be subject to reasonable public regulation. Nevertheless, the resolution exerts a pervasive influence not only on the subjective but also on the objective, external side of the line. The democratic man's complete freedom of thought and his almost complete freedom of discussion serve to liberate not only his inner life but also his social transactions. It is never enough to say that he can merely think what he likes.

For how does the resolution proceed to develop the social regulations that he is expected to obey? By summoning the very mechanisms of thought, conscience, and communication to which it has secured the widest measure of freedom and using them to establish a continual flow of opinion mutually between citizen and citizen and reciprocally between citizenry and officialdom, culminating at intervals in the formal mandates of the ballot box. In this way, when the democratic process operates in accordance with its own specifications, it is able to accomplish much more than even Thomas Jefferson claimed for it. When true to itself, it not only derives the just *powers* of government from the consent of the governed, as he wrote in the Declaration of Independence; it also draws on the governed and their consent to warrant the just *applications and exercises* of the powers. On these terms, law, government, and official compulsion are provided with an unexceptionable moral basis. Freedom of inquiry and discussion on one side and justice of administration on the other are the twin pillars that together support the moral authority of a representative government.

The condition of democratic man is something new and young on the face of the earth, and his work of political creation is only beginning. In all the sad stages of human history, his is the first that, by grace of intelligence, can actually will the elements of a just society into practical existence. Now that he has commenced to discover his capacities and flex his desires, the work is visibly accumulating power and momentum. I see a world where no nation is accounted strong except in justice, rich except in compassion, or secure except in freedom and peace.

# *Notes and References*

CHAPTER I

## THE PURPOSE OF THIS BOOK

The best account of Joe's case is in Jerome Frank and Barbara Frank, *Not Guilty* (New York, Doubleday & Co., Inc., 1957), 17. Further references, *ibid.*, 253.

CHAPTER II

## THE BACKGROUND IN DEMOCRATIC THINKING

*A Consumer Perspective*

Bartkus v. Illinois, 359 U.S. 121 (1959).

It is good to report that Bartkus' case had a happy ending. As he was indigent, the United States Supreme Court appointed a Chicago lawyer by the name of Walter Fisher to represent him without compensation. Mr. Fisher "did a magnificent job both on brief and argument, but to his everlasting credit did not give up when he lost in the Supreme Court." He induced the Illinois state legislature to enact a statute providing that thereafter a verdict of conviction or acquittal in a federal court would bar a trial for the same offense in the courts of Illinois (Ill. Ann. Stat. ch. 38 §601.1). Then, since the statute did not operate retrospectively, Mr. Fisher prevailed on the governor of Illinois to extend its spirit to Bartkus by commuting his sentence to the time already served. In January 1961 Bartkus emerged a free man. Justice William J. Brennan, Jr., of the Supreme Court, who gives me this gratifying information, adds:

"The story is a distinct credit not only to Mr. Fisher but to the entire profession. It is too little understood how lawyers without compensation will make admirable sacrifices of time and energy in order to vindicate the rights of even the worst offenders." A just and proper tribute. Nevertheless, under the decision of the Supreme Court majority, double prosecutions like Bartkus' remain constitutionally permissible in the many *other* states whose laws have not been similarly reformed.

*The Given and the Created*

Weems v. United States, 217 U.S. 349 (1910).

Louisiana ex rel. Francis v. Resweber, 329 U.S. 459 (1947).

Trop v. Dulles, 356 U.S. 86 (1958).

## CHAPTER III
## CITIZENSHIP: COLLECTIVE RESPONSIBILITIES

*Education in Collective Responsibility*

Mr. Morris' case is Berman v. Parker, 348 U.S. 26 (1954). The opinion of the court below is in Schneider v. District of Columbia, 117 F. Supp. 705, 719 (D.C. Dist. of Col. 1953).

The background of Borchard's plan can be found in Senate Documents Vol. 24, S.D. No. 974, 62nd Congress, 3d Session, entitled "State Indemnity for Errors of Criminal Justice" (Dec. 10, 1912).

The federal legislation for reparation of erroneous convictions is: 28 U.S.C. §§1495 and 2513.

For Aristotle's observations on changes in the value of currency, see *Politics* 1306b, 1308b.

Near v. Minnesota, 283 U.S. 697 (1931).

*Responsibility in Community Enterprise*

The New York statute on helping a policeman is Penal Law sec. 1848. For England, see Criminal Law Act 1826, 7 Geo. 4, c. 64, sec. 30.

The New York Tort Claims Act was N.Y. Laws 1929 c. 467. The federal Act is 28 U.S.C. §2671. See *1956 Annual Survey of American Law* 582 for background. It is fair to say that the better courts are hostile to the plea of sovereign immunity, and do their best to circumvent it. Taylor v. New Jersey Highway Authority, 22 N.J. 454, 126 A.2d 313 (1956).

Williams v. New York, 308 N.Y. 548, 127 N.E.2d 545 (1955).

Not long ago, the late Margery Fry, reviving a proposal of Bentham's, urged that the state pay compensation to all victims of criminal violence regardless of the state's having any causal connection with the act of violence. For example, the family of a murdered man would receive compensation whether or not the murderer had escaped from state custody and whether or not he was ever under state control. Though the proposal has had a mixed reception, I believe that suitable legislation could be framed to implement it cautiously, prevent its misuse, and realize its just purposes at least in part. See "Compensation for Victims of Criminal Violence: A Round Table," 8 J. of Pub. L. 191 (1959).

## CHAPTER IV
## CITIZENSHIP: INDIVIDUAL RESPONSIBILITIES

*The Guilt of Accessories*

The Tiberius quotation is from Tacitus' *Annals* bk. IV, xxx.

*The Self-Search in Operation*

See United States ex rel. Knauff v. Shaughnessy, 338 U.S. 537 (1950), and Knauff, *The Ellen Knauff Story* (New York, W. W. Norton & Co., 1952). For the Mezei case, see Shaughnessy v. United States ex rel. Mezei, 345 U.S. 206 (1953). The current statutory law is contained in 8 U.S.C. §1225(c).

## CHAPTER V
## WITHDRAWAL AND ASSOCIATION

*Responsibility and Withdrawal*

Madison's statement appeared in the *National Gazette* on December 19, 1791. Together with other statements of his which are mentioned in this chapter, it may be found in *The Writings of James Madison* (G. Hunt ed., 1906), VI.

The "watchman" passage is from c. 33 of the prophet Ezekiel.

The Hawthorne quotation is from *The House of the Seven Gables*, c. XII.

*Responsibility and Association*

The Fox quotation appears in *The Speeches of Charles James Fox* (London, 1815), V, 289.

The English decision is Martell v. Consett Iron Co. Ltd. [1955] 1 Ch. 363.

National Ass'n for Adv. of Col. P. v. Alabama, 357 U.S. 449 (1958).

CHAPTER VI

## EQUALITY PASSIVE AND ACTIVE

*Passive Equality*

Yick Wo v. Hopkins, 118 U.S. 356 (1886). The 1952 Act amended 12 U.S.C. §1422.

*Active Equality*

The best text on most of the legal aspects of desegregation is J. Greenberg, *Race Relations and American Law* (New York, Columbia University Press, 1959).

The Louisville, Kentucky, case was Buchanan v. Warley, 245 U.S. 60 (1917). The attack on residential segregation was carried much farther in Shelley v. Kraemer, 334 U.S. 1 (1948).

The Missouri case was Missouri ex rel. Gaines v. Canada, 305 U.S. 337 (1938).

For the Dewey anecdote see *Dialogue on John Dewey*, 114 (C. Lamont ed., New York, Horizon Press, Inc., 1959).

For my analysis of the social psychologists' testimony, see *1954 Annual Survey of American Law* 809 (also in 30 N.Y.U.L. Rev. 150) and *1955 Annual Survey of American Law* 655 (also in 31 N.Y.U.L. Rev. 182).

The Texas case was Sweatt v. Painter, 339 U.S. 629 (1950).

The Oklahoma case was McLaurin v. Oklahoma State Regents, 339 U.S. 637 (1950).

The Desegregation Decisions were Brown v. Board of Education of Topeka, 347 U.S. 483 (1954), and Bolling v. Sharpe, 347 U.S. 497 (1954).

*Between Equality and Liberty*

The group-libel law case was Beauharnais v. Illinois, 343 U.S. 250 (1952).

For an instructive study of group-libel legislation in France, see Belton, "The Control of Group Defamation: A Comparative Study of Law and Its Limitations," 34 Tulane L. Rev. 299 (1960).

On state laws against intermarriage, see Justice Roger Traynor's splendid opinion in Perez v. Lippold, 32 Calif. 2d 711, 198 P.2d 17 (1948).

## CHAPTER VII
## QUALITY: THE VIRTUE OF JUDGMENT

*The Search for Quality*

For Aristotle's views on citizen quality, see Politics 1277b, 1296b, and 1327b–1328a. His statements at the beginning of bk. VIII, 1337a, are the ones I would qualify. For Jefferson and Adams, see their letters to each other during the latter half of 1813, most conveniently assembled in *The Adams-Jefferson Letters* (Lester J. Cappon, ed., University of North Carolina Press, 1959).

*Quality in Judgment*

Aristotle's splendid analysis of judgment and prudence is in bk. VI of his *Ethics.*

Due process of decision is discussed in c. IX of *The Moral Decision* (Indiana University Press, 1955).

The fullest statement of Judge Frank's "fact skepticism" is his *Courts on Trial* (Princeton University Press, 1949). For my extrapolations, see "Jerome Frank's Fact-Skepticism and Our Future," 66 Yale L. J. 824 (1957), and "Fact-Skepticism and Fundamental Law," 33 N.Y.U.L. Rev. 1 (1958), also available in *1957 Annual Survey of American Law* 575.

For Locke's notion of grading, see his *Essay,* bk. IV, c. XV. Kant makes an interesting allusion to grading beliefs in terms of lesser and greater wagers, *Critique of Pure Reason* 647 (N. Kemp Smith trans., 1929). In explaining the grading of beliefs, I often use the example of Helvering v. Mitchell, 303 U.S. 376 (1938).

Aristotle's remarks on equity are taken from his *Rhetoric* 1374b.

CHAPTER VIII

## QUALITY: THE VIRTUES OF HONOR AND ASSOCIABILITY

*An Instance of Honor*

Socrates' statements are taken from Plato's *Apology*. Mr. Crossman's comments appear in his *Plato Today* (first published 1937, rev. ed. 1959; Oxford University Press), 59.

*Associability*

Aristotle's discussion of popular judgment is in *Politics* 1281b–1286b.

For Brandeis' unpublished opinions, see *The Unpublished Opinions of Mr. Justice Brandeis: The Supreme Court at Work* (A. M. Bickel ed., Belknap Press, 1957).

The Oklahoma ice case is New State Ice Co. v. Liebmann, 285 U.S. 262 (1932).

CHAPTER IX

## THE REPRESENTATION OF FREE MEN

*The Justice of Administration*

John Dewey's statement may be found in *Intelligence in the Modern World: John Dewey's Philosophy* (J. Ratner ed., Modern Library, 1939), 525.

John Locke's remark appears in his *Essay* bk. II, c. XXI.

In the story of the three foxes, I have considerably amended and elaborated the Aesop fable that was Aristotle's favorite. See *Rhetoric* 1394b.

*Acknowledgment*

Ever since I became a member of the faculty of New York University, Professor Julius Marke, Librarian of the School of Law, has increased the joys and reduced the discomforts of my research by his unfailing cooperation. It is a pleasure to express my grateful appreciation. As every scholar knows, a dedicated librarian is the salt of the earth.

I wish also to thank A. L. Hart, Jr., of The Macmillan Company, for his remarkable understanding and for a brilliant editorial suggestion.

EDMOND CAHN